The Empire's New Clothes

The Empire's New Clothes:
Paradigm Lost, and Regained

Harry Harootunian

PRICKLY PARADIGM PRESS
CHICAGO

Prickly Paradigm Press, LLC
5629 South University Avenue
Chicago, Il 60637

www.prickly-paradigm.com

ISBN: 0-9728196-7-3
LCCN: 2004112108

Printed in the United States of America on acid-free
paper.

"But we must return… to the most important promise made by modernization: its evenness. Modernization is even because it holds within itself a theory of spatial and temporal convergence: all societies will come to look like us, all will arrive eventually at the same stage or level, all the possibilities of the future are being lived now, at least for the West: there they are, arrayed before us, a changeless world functioning under the sign of technique… Modernization promises a perfect reconciliation of past and future in an endless present, a world where all sedimentation of social experience has been leveled or smoothed away, where poverty has been reabsorbed, and, most important, a world where class conflict is a thing of the past, the strains of contradiction washed out in a superhuman hygienic effort, by new levels of abundance and equitable distribution."

Kristin Ross, *Fast Cars, Clean Bodies*

"Above all, the new concepts offered hope. No doubt Africa had never invented the wheel, no doubt Asian religions were fatalist, no doubt Islam preached submission, no doubt Latins combined racial miscegenation with a lack of entrepreneurial thrift; but it could now be asserted that these failings were not biological, merely cultural. And if, like the Japanese, the underdeveloped were clever enough to invent an indigenous version of Calvinism, or if they could be induced to change the content of their children's readers (the children first being taught to read, of course), or if transistors were placed in remote villages, or if farsighted elites mobilized benighted masses with the aid of altruistic outsiders, or if…, then underdevelopment too would cross the river Jordan and come into a land flowing with milk and honey. This was the hope offered up by the modernization theorists."

Immanuel Wallerstein, "Modernization: *requiescat in pace*"

I: PARADIGM'S EMPIRE

The purpose of this little book is admirably condensed in the two opening quotations. I would like to situate my observations on modernization theory between them and consider the paradigm's history as it was formulated in the early years of the Cold War to eventually authorize an agenda for developing the non-aligned nations of the old East and the new South that had just recently emerged from decolonization. During these years immediately after the conclusion of World War II, the United States and the Soviet Union engaged in a titanic contest to win the allegiance of new nation states to their respective models of modernity and development. As a theory of social change, modernization thrust the social sciences, at least in the United States, onto a world stage these disciplines had not previously known that led to designing a methodological program based on comparison. By the same measure the formation of a theory of modernizing new societies (those that had not yet attained some requisite level of modernity) implicated social scientists, on a scale never before imagined, in state policy to become what the historian Loren Baritz once named the "servants of power." With an undying faith in the instrumentality of a means/end rationality, itself never far from its source in economic theory, social science envisaged how newly emerged nations might be able to modernize peacefully, especially after the often traumatic passage out of colonization, rather than through an alternative strategy that recommended revolutionary violence to overcome the distance between their current circum-stances and the rich industrial societies of Euro-America.

The developmentalism contrived to transform "traditional" societies into modern, rational nations was principally spearheaded by the effort to induce newly founded nations, usually former colonies, to fashion their societies in such a way as to be receptive to American products, even though its ideological representation invariably projected a benevolently altruistic and liberal desire to offer a "helping hand." The programs aimed to persuade new nations to commit their political economies to marketization and democratization with often disastrous results. What was at the heart of modernization theory and its promise for practical application, and why its exemplars are still relevant to understanding the current situation, was the desire to promote political stabilization among the new nations after decolonization as a condition for implementing economic development fueled by the market. While marketization invariably swelled the wealth of a minority, democratization enfranchised whole populations only to put control back into the hands of elites (often linked to the rich), as the case of Japan's long-standing "single-party democracy" amply demonstrates. Japan, of course, is the one country that had been constantly held up as the most successful model of capitalist modernization of "late-comer" nations in the "free-world." This imaginary was produced by social scientists and historians in the 1960s and 1970s, with generous support from America's leading philanthropic foundations, who thus created a large literature determined to showing how the Japanese experience conformed to normative theories of social change and conceptions of development. I will turn to this literature later and examine how its claims of political stabilization and economic growth were made to appear as exemplary experiences worthy of emulation by unaligned societies in the era of the Cold War. The advantage of the Japanese example over the model of American society was clearly its location in Asia and its geographic (though not temporal) proximity to the Third World. Even attempts to adjust the rate of marketization and democratization, in order to allow time for the adaptation to, and absorption of, necessary change, by envisaging stages of tutelage and transition, failed to keep in check the very excesses the paradigm of modernization was supposed to eliminate from tradition-bound societies. The disparity between the signature of modernity, namely a developmental program bringing about capitalist consumption, and the local circumstance this was designed to transform could never actually be closed or even directly acknowledged, despite the well meaning efforts of liberal social science in those years. What modernization discourse managed to accomplish was a displacement of capitalism by something called "modernity" and the processes conceived for realizing it. A good deal of theory was expended in an attempt to show that modernity, as opposed to merely capitalism, meant satisfying a rational outlook that would lead to a greater control of nature, differentiation and specialization as preconditions for the even greater integration of society. Whose rationality and for whom were questions never asked.

Wallerstein recognized early on that the world of the postwar was not about achievement, as such, but profit. But once "achievement" was fixed as both the law of rationality and the criterion of the modernizing process, social sciences rushed to establish comparisons of incommensurable magnitude as the standard of measurement, even though the instance of unevenness not only derived from the extension of capitalism but was necessary for its continual reproduction. It was less the absence of exercising a means/end rationality successfully that dogged the modernizing efforts of new nations and kept them permanently from reaching the promised stage of convergence than the necessity of capitalism to create unevenness as a condition of its own expansion. The paradigm of modernization thus provided a checklist for how societies could satisfy a number of requirements to become "modern;" it also told them of their location in the cosmic grid of progress. While this program flourished throughout the Cold War, and was inseparable from it, its commitment to rationality exceeded its conviction in comparative measurement. Once the Cold War ended, social science threw out the bath water but kept the baby, or vice versa, and turned back to a purely formalistic rationality itself, no longer constrained by a concern with culture, society, and history, no longer in need of comparative frameworks and the action of historically and culturally derived value systems and their differences. The only things that seemed to count were preferences and decisions based on either rationally calculated expectations promising a maximization of choice or those that failed to measure up. Under these circumstances, the only worthwhile comparison was one that observed the difference between success or failure, maximizing interest or not, and that comparison could be made anywhere in a world "unified" by capitalism.

Finally, I want also to suggest that even though modernization as a theory of social change disappeared with the closing down of competition and the collapse of the Soviet Union, it has reappeared in the guise of a celebratory new imperialism of rational achievements now attributed to the historical empires and the lessons they hold for the contemporary American imperium. But before we specify this connection it is important to provide an account of what might be called the imperial return in the current circumstances of contemporary history.

II: TAILING EMPIRE

Since 9/11, there has been a quickening of the return of imperialism in popular discourse and an ever increasing circulation of terms like "empire" in newspapers, TV talk shows, and even drama describing America's current global involvements. Although an awareness of American imperial aspirations had already been recorded by critics and commentators before the fateful destruction of the World Trade Center in New York City, the recent and aggressive re-surfacing of imperialism as both an older, historical category and as a concept and description employed in contemporary political discussion and scholarly opinion constitutes an event of such overdetermined magnitude that it is now threatening to exceed even 9/11 as a symptom of what it says about our current situation. Everywhere one turns these days *imperialism* and *empire* seem to crop up. As far as I know, empire and imperialism have not yet been appropriated for naming a new perfume. Rather, their ubiquity is more reminiscent of the return of the repressed, what had always been there but hidden in the recesses of the political and cultural unconscious, lurking in nameless anonymity yet ready to explode to remind us of what we had "forgotten." Not too long ago, during the now barely remembered Gulf War of 1990-91, it was rare to see political commentary and analyses resort to the category of imperialism to explain American military intervention to save what all agreed was little more than a Kuwaiti gas station, even though the rhetoric constantly insisted that the U.S. forces had been deployed to save democracy in a monarchical form from Iraqi oppression.

Unsurprisingly, the same appeal to the imperative of democratization is making the rounds again to legitimate American purpose in Iraq and Afghanistan as templates, albeit as yet incomplete ones, for structural change throughout the entire region. But this proclamation echoes an earlier sentiment that demanded programs of development, materialized in offering aid and assistance exported to uncommitted new nations of the Third World during the Cold War. It might be recalled that the explicit goal of developmentalism sought to yoke capitalist economic growth with political democracy, linking the two as a natural coupling and thus defining the vocation of development itself which aimed to concretize an elaborate theory of modernization and convergence designed by American social science in the immediate post-war years. The willingness to use military force was never far from the desire to realize this mission and the "imperial" dictates of the modernizing paradigm which war in Vietnam amply illustrated. I will return to explaining its figuration later but for now it is important to say more about the contemporary discussion on imperialism and empire.

Part of this renewed interest in imperialism and the status of America's empire no doubt stems from the decision to intervene in Afghanistan in the wake of 9/11 to settle the score with the terrorist base that launched the attack. Subsequent drumbeating by the Bush administration, designed to whip the population into a frenzied and patriotic fervor and even hysteria according to color coded "security" emergencies, sought to create unquestioning support for decisive action in a "war on terrorism" that had no exit or temporal terminus. All this prefigured the actual invasion of Iraq in March 2003. In the context of these new military adventures, a context that included criticism leveled by both domestic demonstrations protesting an immanent war and foreign opposition to unilateral action raised by some of the United States' G-8 partners, it is not unreasonable to see the implacable drift of war as simply a sign of imperial ambition. Despite the reluctance of left/liberals to voice the i-word to describe what Washington has plainly been planning all along (the same kind of squeamishness inhibits the use of "fascism" to label the political form recent policies have assumed to justify intervention and what recently has been described as the "militarization of everyday life" in the United States), even the Bush administration's principal spokespersons and fellow travelers have had no qualms in finally calling a spade a spade by labeling the action of the United States as an expression of imperialism in a new register.

As early as November 2001 Richard Haass—currently President of the Council of Foreign Relations and at the time soon-to-be appointed director of policy planning in the State Department under President George W. Bush (Bush II)—delivered a now notoriously famous paper titled, "Imperial America." In it he outlined what the United States would have to do to achieve global prominence in the post-Cold War era. To realize a new hegemony, the United States would be obliged to "re-conceive their role from traditional nation-state to an 'imperial power.'" Even though Haass assiduously avoided using the term *imperialism* when describing America's new global vocation, as if doing so brought a grant of immunity, he wanted, nevertheless, to emphasize that the former (imperial power), unlike the latter (imperialism), implied no territorial ambitions and commercial exploitation. Indeed, Haass may very well have been thinking of a "benevolent empire" used earlier and elsewhere to portray Japan's oppressive seizure and colonization of Korea after the Russo-Japanese war of 1904-05. Like others after him, Haass was proposing that imperial America represented an empire without colonies or, perhaps worse, Hardt and Negri's acephalic empire of the multitude, whose truncated figure appeared at about the same moment to announce the return of empire and offer something for everybody. Here is Haass:

> The U.S. role would resemble 19th century Great Britain...coercion and force would be the last resort; what was written by John Gallagher and Ronald Robinson 50 years ago about Great Britain that "British policy followed the principle of extending control informally if possible and formally if necessary" could be applied to the American role at the start of the new century.

The real problem, as he saw it, was to worry about "what to do with a surplus of power and the many and considerable advantages this confers on the United States." This reference to surplus reflected, above all else, the inordinate domination of the world's military represented by the United States (40%), its obsessive monopolization of military power that now equals a force greater than the next eight powers put together (and by some measures greater than all countries combined), with a budget equal to the next twelve to fifteen countries. Haass probably recognized that in the comparison with the British Empire of the nineteenth century, American military power appears infinitely greater and better equipped than Britain's paltry overseas strike force. Yet, as he and others constantly remind us, this overwhelming military superiority is designed neither to expropriate territory, as such, nor even to defeat rivals (now that the Soviet Union has been eliminated), seeking no territorial acquisitions or control of trade routes reminiscent of earlier imperial ventures. Disproportionate military capacity, unmotivated by the desire for coercion, capable of extending anywhere, sustaining two or three fronts at once, has no clear and finite objectives that would require its application. Summoning the historical analogy to "normalize" America's imperium has become today one of the leading rhetorical devices enabling current discussions on the status of empire. Haass' choice of the British Empire has become the staple of a number of contemporary discourses whose punctual and repetitive airing littering the pages of *The New York Times*—serving more these days as a willing mouthpiece and stenographer of the state than as a purveyor of "all the news that's fit to print"—

works to remind readers both of the necessity of an American Empire and its developmental imperative to spread democracy everywhere at any cost. Right wing propagandists like Max Boot (a current fellow of the Council on Foreign Relations) and the ideological gun for hire Niall Ferguson openly ape Haass' earlier recommendation by offering reassurances that the current American adventure, like its British model, can be done cheaply.

Haass' insistence that the empire is guided neither by a desire to use force nor an aptitude for territorial acquisition departs from the very model he has embraced, and defies, therefore, both the history produced by the British Empire since the eighteenth century and, as I will show below, the more recent history of America's recuperation of its pattern since the end of World War II. By announcing that the United States has no interest in deploying force unless necessary Haass is, in fact, raising its prospect without enumerating the conditions prompting such a decision. We know now, of course, that no explanation need be given other than the reason of empire itself, which unintentionally confirms the observation made years ago by Nikos Poulantzas, amending a phrase from Max Horkheimer, that "anyone who does not wish to discuss imperialism should stay silent on the subject of fascism." But the force of its reverse is equally true and those who wish to talk about imperialism today cannot remain silent on the question of fascism. The vision of America's empire people like Haass have advanced resembles an invisible, moral universe—a cross between Stefan Georg's mystical, "hidden Germany" and Hardt and Negri's nameless and headless abode of the multitude. Moreover, Haass was worried at the time of his speech that the United States might fail to rise and meet the challenge of seizing this opportunity and thus squander the opportunity to "bring about a world supportive of its interests" by doing too little, too late. This argument for embedding "core interests" as the propelling agent in achieving global economic domination and "democratization" by unimagined military might reiterates the sentiment of Robert Cooper, a Tony Blair loyalist, when he proposed a revival of nineteenth-century distinctions that supplied imperialism with moral and cultural purpose. The characteristics he had in mind were those that had differentiated between civilized, barbarian, and savage states but relocated in a revised register of modern and pre-modern, with the post-modern now acting as custodian of civilized conduct and inducing, through direct or indirect subordination, compliance with universal norms and humanistic practices across the breadth of the globe. While this language relied on an older binary that often evoked earlier associations of civilization and barbarism, it more frequently reflected the imperial idiom of a bygone age and willingly risks what the tender-hearted today refer to as political incorrectness.

Cooper's refashioning of older categories into modern and non-modern reverberates with echoes of America's relentless liberal moral mission for modernizing the unaligned new nations in order to win them over for democracy and capitalism during the Cold War epoch. Recalling Haass' reference to the pursuit of embedded core interests, the modernization agenda, as we shall see, had already sought to promote the core economic interests of the United States as a developmental imperative. This explains why the Cold War seemed so overdetermined in the United States, and why its concept appeared as America's principal export to the rest of the world— especially those countries outside of Euro-America where hot wars were regularly being fought. Samuel Huntington, no stranger to modernization theory, has recently reworked this program into the familiar clash of civilizations, while the current mayor of Tokyo, Ishihara Shintaro, has nominated Japan to be the eastern flank of this new imperial formation no longer devoted to modernizing but to defending the core. Huntington's representation situates the United States as the proxy for the West and thus its leading custodian in the forthcoming collision of civilizations, while Ishihara has called the adversaries of order and profit "Third Nations," obviously implying the distant but still vivid and discredited figure of the Third World (specifically applied to Second World countries like the People's Republic and North Korea) and thereby sustaining the diminished anti-communist fervor of the Cold War. As whacky as this scenario seems, it comes very close to the mission the American military is presently committing its energies to realizing. For there can be no denying that the declared war against terrorism simply continues the earlier struggle against underdevelopment and back-wardness (renamed barbarism) in the name of modern civilization. In fact, it is a recuperation of the Cold

War in a different register and "rubric," as William Grieder has recently observed in *The Nation*.

Irving Kristol—whose apparent five minutes on the left as a student at CCNY in the last century has qualified him to speak endlessly and authoritatively during a lifetime for the right on the dangers he has "experienced"—has proposed the astonishing idea that the United States has become an imperial nation because it has been invited to be so (an argument used widely these days). As Kristol put it a few years ago, "the world wanted it to happen, needed it to happen," by orchestrating a string of "relatively minor crises that could be resolved by...American involvement." The political commentator Michael Igantieff has no hesitation proposing, on every possible occasion, that empire is the only word capable of describing present day America's global entanglements, even though in a recent book he has pulled back somewhat and called it "Empire lite." Thomas Friedman, who habitually calls one thing by another name, constantly employs "globalization" in order to displace what plainly looks and quacks like imperialism and older forms of modernization promoted under American tutelage. Andrew Bacevich, a conservative by any count, believes only a "sight-stopping astigmatism" and the aversion to identify naked self-interest prevents us from using the term imperialism to describe what are clearly manifest American aspirations. Finally, in the gallery of usual right wing suspects, the redoubtable and ever available for a fee Richard Perle has referred to the "war on terrorism" as "total war" and by extension "infinite war." The last time the concept of "total war" was seriously employed was by the Japanese as they prepared for their own drive for empire in China and Southeast Asia. But as the Japanese so plainly showed, the idea of total war was conceived to mobilize the whole of domestic society and prepare it to wage warfare indefinitely, if necessary, to secure control of an economic zone called the East Asia Co-Prosperity Sphere, another name for empire. Here is the real meaning of Poulantzas' rephrasing of Horkheimer and its chilling lesson for contemporary American society. Moreover, we know, too, that in this regard "total" or "infinite" war meant preparedness and a willingness to deploy force unilaterally and pre-emptively, as both Japan's war in Pacific Asia and America's attack on Iraq illustrate. What this current imperial return requires is a reconsideration of its meaning in light of an earlier historical experience and its relationship to the contemporary manifestation.

Reawakening to the Meaning of Imperialism

We must be careful not to allow ourselves to be recuperated by an optic that sees no further than contemporary or current events. Immediacy cannot provide an instant illumination of the order of events empowered to reveal a larger explanation of what is happening before our eyes. This optic, in and of itself, was perhaps inspired by the categorization of the Cold War itself (and the construction of "international relations" as an academic discipline). Current discussions of America's imperial role, it seems to me, rely too hurridly on the immediate configuration instead of more distantly mediated and mediating associations that might help resituate contemporary history in a broader context. In the present day scramble for meaning, it is possible to observe two responses that derive their force from the immediate political environment and contemporary discussions that seek to move beyond its presentist horizon. Both remind us of an earlier history and the attempts to account for and explain the sources motivating imperialist activity and its larger meaning. Firstly, a Marxian return to the question after a long dormancy that now wishes to identify the structural "dysfunctions" of capital; and secondly what we might call a new, old historicist representation that wants to demonstrate how the experience of prior empires has been more beneficial than hitherto imagined for the future of former colonies. The latter representation manages to supply support, directly or indirectly (depending on one's politics), to the trajectory of contemporary American imperialism. While I will say more about this further on, I want to suggest here that its historicist claims fuses a Rankean conviction that judges the intention of earlier imperialists and colonizers to an authoritative confirmation founded on the Hegelian "cunning of reason." In the case of its most extreme practitioner, Niall Ferguson, it is a confident positivism harnessed to the fantasy of a counterfactual "what might have been" that immediately acquires the status of "should be" identified with a "what is." In any case, bad historicisms. But both of these recent exercises to historicize contemporary American imperial adventures constitute a shadowing which, like a private eye, tracks down and even stalks the movements of empire for its meaning. At its heart stands Hardt and Negri, whose *Empire* unintentionally plays the swing function (a revolving door effect?) of mediating between both perspectives, inasmuch as it tries to satisfy two contradictory positions. (1) To the Marxian desire to account for the structural dysfunctions of capital that have led to contemporary imperialism, it offers the vision of a different kind of empire, discontinuous from its historical antecedents, with its displacement of economics by politics that shifts discussion over to the domain of sovereignty (and to a Foucauldian preoccupation with "governmentality") to ultimately substitute a revolutionary model for an evolutionary one. But Hardt and Negri manage only to recuperate an older theory of modernization that is now made to show how "globalization" has diminished the power of the nation-state to the extent that neither the United States nor indeed any other country today "form the center of the imperialist project," as they put it. (2) For the celebratory historicist rediscovery of a good, old imperialism and its influentially long term benefits *Empire* has given the imperial form a new lease on life in the current conjuncture at the same time that it has gotten the U.S. off the hook by refusing to name it.

On occasion Hardt and Negri's conception of empire comes close to resembling Kautsky's "ultra imperialism," inasmuch as its form constitutes a league-like configuration that incorporates nation-states. Moreover, *Empire* shares with contemporary discussions of current events an astonishing insensitivity to history, to any historicism, good, bad, or simply indifferent (a strange blindness even for "neo-Marxists"). *Empire*'s program has proven to be not only out of step with its moment but its projection of an already headless imperial configuration enabled by globalization has merely transferred the older requirements of a once declared dead theory of modernization to a new level of promised convergence—the global completion of the commodity relation.

But Hardt and Negri's book signaled a reawakening to imperialism at the meta-theoretical level, a concern for empire and the imperial formation among the Marxist left. Marxian theories of imperialism, it is worth recalling, had once constituted one of the principal mainstays of the discourse. By the time the Berlin Wall came down in 1989, bringing with it the rubble of "actually existing socialism" in Eastern Europe, Marxian theories of imperialism had already run their course and played out their productivity. During its long history, Marxian modes of analysis have, I believe, been plagued by a fundamental ambivalence over (and perhaps a contest between) the claims pressed by a theory of modernization that has had difficulty in differentiating between two, often contradictory desires: those centered on the achievement of socialism and those propelled by the desire of "catching up" with capitalism. The latter impulse was immensely exacerbated by and during the Cold War era and was probably furthered by the exportation of bourgeois-liberal ideas of development and modernization's promise of convergence. This particular move often sacrificed a Marxian critique of the commodity form and its consequences—that is, a critique of the categories of the base of capitalist modernization for one that targeted only their distribution and application. What I mean is that for more than a century, Marxian thought had served a theory of modernization by failing to promote a critique based on evaluating the status of the commodity fetish as the structuring principal of society (what Marx called the "germinal cell") rather than merely its superstructural ideology. With this orientation as a guiding principle, parties and workers' organizations have together contributed to their own integration into capitalist society, all the while seeking to liberate the latter from its anachronisms and structural deficiencies. In the capitalist periphery, from Russia to Africa and Asia, Marxian thought was employed to justify the late modernization of those societies. Traditional Marxists, whether Leninist or social democrats, academicians or revolutionaries, socialists or Third Worldists, promoted the struggle for the redistribution of income, commodities and value, without putting their order of importance into question, at the expense of class conflict. In retrospect, it can probably now be argued that the entirety of the traditional Marxian theoretical program and its practical applications in both the "actually existing socialist" countries and the Western industrial social democracies constituted only an element in the development of commodity society. The global crisis of capitalism and globalization itself is nothing more than a fleeting moment in the advance of capitalism, which pointed to a crisis of Marxism itself. We must, in any case, envisage Marxian theories of imperialism as an outgrowth of a tendency to project a conception of modernization that will, at the same time, supply a critique capable of competing with the capitalist version. Theories of imperialism were mediated by the historical specificity of these conflicting demands at any given moment.

For our purposes it might be convenient to propose that the production of these theories were distributed between a Luxemburgian emphasis on the role played by the primitive accumulation of capital, the Kautskyan identification of "ultra imperialism," and the Leninist formulation that ratcheted imperialism to the "highest or latest stage of capitalism." This division inevitably generated the conditions for a collision between a view that necessitated geographical and imperial expansion to solve the crisis of surplus (Luxemburg), one that envisioned imperialism leading to an era of peace both in the "national" class struggle and among nation states through the agreements of a world imperial formation (Kautsky), and an analysis that imagined imperialism as a further aggravation of capitalist contradictions on a global scale, in new and intensified form, leading to a new stage of world conflict (Lenin). Yet, all the stake seemed to share was the importance accorded to large-scale structural determinants that would necessitate the construction of a periodization scheme and a proper "stage-ist" chronology that brought in its train "crisis," "economic catastrophism," "contradictions," etc. In all of these theorizations of imperialism, the role of the state remained relatively recessive, as did the question of the reproduction of unevenness as a principal constituent of the capitalist mode of production in the development of imperialism. When Marxists turned to rethinking the question of imperialism, at the moment in the 1990s when it became evident that history had not yet evaporated, they revived this structural conceit, and its accompanying assumption that the leading economic elements will disaggregate to bring down the capitalist system. But what writers added to their analyses of structural implosion was the figure of the nation-state, especially its economic role initiating internationalization. With David Harvey, there is the additional recognition of uneven geographic development and the reproduction of capitalism through "accumulation by dispossession," an updating of primitive accumulation.

What is so important about recent Marxian re-evaluations is the repetition of the explanatory primacy granted to structural causality and its scheme of periodization. Hence, one current analysis (by Peter Gowan) describes "Washington's Faustian" bid as a bold, global gamble, stemming from the way in which international monetary and financial relations have been refigured and managed over the past 25 years. Moreover, this redesigning has resulted in specific political choices made by the United States—globalization as "state policy-dependency phenomena"—and the construction of an economic regime to serve as the instrument of economic statecraft and power politics. The "Dollar Wall Street Regime" originated in the early 1970s with Nixon's decision to abandon the

Bretton Woods agreement and let the dollar float against other currencies and his willingness to make a deal with the Saudis to drive up the price of oil. Another account put forth by Leo Panitch and Sam Ginden has demanded the fashioning of a new Marxian theory of imperialism that will exceed the constraints of the older stage-ist narrative and its reliance on inter-imperial rivalry in order to address those factors that have led to "America's informal empire." Specifically, this new theorization, recalling the earlier formulations of Nikos Poulantzas, foregrounds the state's capacity to incorporate rivals in the "imperial chain" and police the globalization process—spreading capitalist social relations everywhere. This strategy shared a family resemblance with an older aspiration prompted by modernization theory during the Cold War. But the state's history in this reincarnation is localized in a Neo-Liberal reconfiguration expressed in such devices as "foreign direct investment." Panitch and Ginden, like Gowan, see the critical inaugural moment of this transmutation in the late 1970s with the "Volcker Shock" which reflected the American state's self-imposed disciplining in a structural adjustment program initiated by the Federal Reserve's decision to establish economic restraints by allowing interest rates to rise to unprecedented levels. For Ellen M. Wood, the new imperial America must be grasped against a backdrop of historical imperialism, to be sure, but is now marked by a global economy whose structural contradictions are sustained by multiple states, in which the extra-economic force of military power, what she calls "surplus imperialism," has become essential to the expansion of the imperium in a wholly new way.

In a recent book on "neo-imperialism," David Harvey concentrates on capitalism's cycle of accumulation crises (recurring surplus labor power and capital), once resolved by what he has described as the "spatial fix"—geographical expansion, now stemming from overproduction since the 1970s. In this connection Peter Gowan has also seen the same moment and the orchestration of volatility by the U.S. as a desperate attempt to preserve its hegemonic position which, according to Wood, would explain the obsessive monopolization of military power that has taken place in the last decades of the twentieth century. Harvey has called the tactic motoring an accelerated imperialism—one that belongs to the order of finance capital rather than mere territorial expropriation—"accumulation by dispossession," a term that retains much of Luxemburg's conception of "primitive accumulation." "Accumulation by dispossession," above all else, refers to predatory practices outside of the capitalist system —theft—that actually resemble extractive operations already in use within the United States, practices that reinforce the currently rampant unevenness shadowing society. But the casino capitalism, Ponzi schemes and pyramid scams, not to forget state lotteries and the like have nothing on the looting of the S & L's and contemporary corporate corruption. A diversity of familiar predatory schemes have been employed by American economic power to fuel its own imperialism in the effort to solve the recurring crises of accumulation that simply result in exacerbating greater unevenness throughout the globe. Yet Harvey, along with others, has still not distanced his own discourse sufficiently from one that has organized capitalism in successive stages leading to collapse or catastrophic implosion. He has not exorcised the ghostly conviction that the state, now armed to the teeth, might conceivably wither away. It is important to recognize in these more recent Marxian theories of imperialism that they still rely on the primacy of stages and its inevitable chronology. This reliance is reflected in their unmarked consensus to locate the source of the current crisis in the 1970s, a gesture which has made the decade into a fateful watershed but one safely within the temporal confines of America's Cold War.

The consensus is, in fact, driven in part by the category of the Cold War itself, and indissolubly linked to its ideological defense of the "rise of the West." What I am suggesting is that this chronology marking the inevitable progression of stage-ism is actually bonded to the nation-state, a category it unproblematically presupposes, rather than to the itinerary of capitalism itself which both intersects with the nation and exceeds it through expansion. It still seems to have more to do with the West, as such, than the Rest. This emphasis was always at the heart of Cold War strategies, just as the staging of hot wars elsewhere in Asia, Africa, or Latin America constituted a principal condition by which the category of Cold War was enabled and managed to sustain its empirical existence. While it is undoubtedly the event of 9/11 and the adventures of the American state that have recharged Marxism to reassess the phenomenon of current imperial formation, confidence in structures and periodization actually work to displace historical analyses to produce a myopic vision that easily overlooks the historicity of more distant moments like the immediate post-World War II years. Moreover, this blindness, which has nothing to do with opposing the usual fetishization of origins, too often ignores the task of interrogating the Cold War itself as a problematic category that frequently functioned to masquerade the promotion of what then were called core economic interests and divert scrutiny away from what clearly were the formative moments of an imperialist impulse *avant la lettre*. To compensate for this historical nearsightedness today there has been the additional effort to envisage historical imperialisms in light of their subsequent legacies for new decolonized societies and as models that might be deployed to refigure the contemporary American imperium.

At the same moment the conjuncture has begun to give rise to a renewed Marxian critique of imperialism we also stand witness to a steadily growing enunciation of its historical legacy and the enduring consequences for the subsequent modernization of former colonies. The interest of this discourse lies in showing that historical imperialism and colonialism, despite chalking up a baneful record of influence throughout Asia and Africa, have surpassed their inaugural moment to intentionally produce lasting contributions to the formation and shape of new nation states after colonization. Even though the renewed effort to rethink imperial and colonial legacies after decolonization began before 9/11, it has been energized by recent events and has stepped up its own pace of production to the extent that its "leading" findings have become part of an everyday common sense doxa found everywhere in the mass media. What this historiographical revival seeks to demonstrate is how imperialism and colonialism, in spite of the acknowledged oppression they inflicted on Africa and Asia, the immense appropriations and dispossessions they visited upon much of the world, and their active undermining of political economies and destruction of received cultures of reference, nevertheless introduced the benefits of modern civilization in the new form of political organization (that is to say, systems able to deliver political stabilization), "governmentalities," and economic arrangements leading to the installation of infrastructural investments that would be later seen to have incalculable effects for the development of the new nation state. (Roland Barthes once called this kind of argument the "margarine effect.") During the early years of the Cold War it was a commonplace to point to Indian "democracy" as a legacy of British colonialism in the emerging struggle for the hearts and minds of the unaligned new nations. Even Japan's prewar imperialist state was made to appear as a model of political rationality, inasmuch as it equipped colonies like Korea and Formosa with a lasting modern infrastructure. Where, in fact, this argument has been used earliest and most persuasively by social scientists and historians is the case of the colonies of the former Japanese empire and their "miraculous" postwar and post-colonial transformations made possible by the infrastructures directly established by

Japan's colonial authority and Japanese direct investment in the development of Formosa and Korea.

   This experience, as we shall see, has relied on
a muscular model of Japan which, in the Cold War
days, was hoisted up by social scientists and historians
as an inspiring exemplar of evolutionary modernization and a mirror for developing "new nations" to
follow. Closer to home, certain imperial powers like
Great Britain were considered to have been
presciently responsible for introducing or inducing in
their colonies private investment and the benefits of
the law (turning extraterritoriality into a civilizational
virtue) and indeed the category of the nation-state
itself, albeit its bourgeois avatar. The reappearance of
an older theory of development, called modernization
and convergence theory, and its re-articulation in
scholarly literature represents a form of overdetermined compensation for the commanding role played
by post-colonial discourse. Everywhere these days, it
seems, a new respect is being lavishly accorded to the
historical empires of the past for their foresight in
shaping the future: the old Russian Czarist Empire,
the Hapsburg, and even the Ottoman imperial config-
urations have all been extolled as mirror models for
later multiculturalism!

   This new, old historiography, now drawing its
energy from the Iraq war and America's imperial policies, represents an assault on the post-colonial desire
to re-narrativize the colonial experience by emphasizing its repressive and disabling legacies and the way in
which the colonized were robbed of subjective recognition and an historical representation of their own

making (the "Provincializing Europe" effect). To offset this "blindness," post-colonial discourse has addressed the question of how the colonized were able to formulate subject positions and act to play a greater role than hitherto imagined in making the relationship between ruler and ruled something more than one between subject and object and a one way street.

It is important to recognize that the contemporary conjuncture has produced a new "respect" for imperialism, in an exaggerated form now constituted by the fusion of an older theory of development, made possible by a paradigm promising modernization and convergence, and the recurrent reaction to post-colonial theory, its critique of the colonial experience and, above all, its claim on the future after decolonization. With modernization in the 1960s and 1970s, especially, a theory of social change promoted by a liberal social science to account for the world outside Euro-America was joined to a program of development dedicated to exporting democracy and capitalism as a natural coupling to win over the non-aligned countries during the Cold War. In fact, the term capitalism was rarely, if ever, used; its substitutes, democracy or modernity, suggested goals which the modernizing process promised to realize. While modernization emphasized both political and economic spheres, its effacement of capitalism for modernity, as such, reflected a conviction that upheld the primacy of political organization—the nation-state form—and the availability of rational leadership over economic development, as, in fact, the necessary condition for capitalist growth and market expansion. In this respect, modernization theory echoed an earlier (and later) Marxist conceit that presupposed the primacy and existence of the nation-state as the agent of economic change, rather than the trajectory of capitalist expansion itself as the principle and principal mediating political form. Driven ceaselessly by a conception of evolutionary growth, more Spencerian than historicist, privileging the survival of vestiges, values, and residues from the past, it often labored to identify prescription with description, a what ought to be with what actually is. To secure scientific authority for its analysis it not only made the world the object of inquiry but mandated comparison as its standard of measurement. In this way, modernization theory continued and sustained a long-standing practice in social science that had eschewed the force of mixed and uneven historical temporalizations for timeless, unilinear structural regularities and enduring patterns of values. In other words, a process without any history.

After the Cold War, modernization's language of prescriptive imperatives was utilized to account for America's arrogation of greater global responsibility for policing, now that the Soviet Union had been eliminated from the field of competition, and intervening wherever "democracy" and "market" were imperiled, which usually meant masking a perceived challenge to "core interests." With the removal of a "real" or "natural" enemy, the contest to win over the hearts and minds no longer prevailed and the urgency of exporting development was replaced by the necessity of exporting democracy as a pre-emptive measure and the best guarantee of political stability, despite prevailing, received sovereignties, as the current Iraqi expedition shows. It should not be surprising that the strategy of pre-emptive war was already worked out in the earlier "war against drugs" which has provided no measurable success, just as the conceptualization of terror derived from the American practice in the latter days of the Cold War to sponsor terroristic groups as proxies in Africa, Central and Latin America, and the Middle East, notably Afghanistan and the struggle to extricate Soviet control. One need only remember the elder Bush's strange history with the Panamanian dictator Noriega, now in a U.S. prison, and the photograph from palmier days of the current Secretary of Defense Donald Rumsfeld shaking hands with a one time ally of the United States, Saddam Hussein, also in custody.

The reaction to post-colonial discourse and its widespread institutionalization (scratch an English department and you'll find a post-colonial outpost) has been enhanced by the desire to demonstrate the great contributions made by the colonizing powers now that they have passed into the precinct of memory and nostalgia and now that the "historical experience" after decolonization has become heritage. The proponents of this counterattack against the entrenched bastions of post-colonial discourse have been enabled by appropriating from modernization theory its obsessive emphasis on the residue of surviving values used to facilitate the modernization process as an evolutionary progression, as, in fact, the agent of social change leading to the achievement of modern nationhood. Earlier practitioners of modernization theory appealed

to a presumed (and indefensible) binary between traditional and modern, the "then" and "now" sequences in
a continuist temporal series characterized notably by
the velocity of change or distance covered by a society
in becoming modern, and to the adaptive capacity of
survivors of the former to help negotiate the accomplishment of the latter. More recent producers of
imperial blather identify the colonial moment as the
instigation of a history that could only lead to the
subsequent modernization of former colonized societies into modern nation-states. In a certain sense this
argumentation resembles a reversal of Bruno Latour's
famous formulation announcing that "we have never
been modern," inasmuch as the colonial inheritance
would now be made to function in such a way as to
show that colonies were always modern, since they
were sent on this itinerary with the advent of the colonizing power. Current efforts to democratize
Afghanistan and Iraq, which means Americanizing
these societies as was done earlier in Japan and West
Germany, still reflect the modernizing impulse of an
earlier time, but without the necessity of disguising
the promotion of core interests since the contest that
once propelled it has ended. Moreover, the recent
maneuver to "democratize" the world pre-emptively
through military intervention unconstrained by
competing rival powers no longer relies on the service
of social science and its comparative strategies to
configure its agenda but rather on a watered-down
mix of Spenglerian theorizing on civilizations and
varieties of Schmidtian and Straussian distrust for
substantive democracy. In fact, the (Leo) Straussian

waltz has been the melody the current Washington administration is humming and the music of choice for the dress balls represented by Iraq and Afghanistan. What we have now is simply a form of political modernization that will make such societies receptive to market forces and American consumer products that scarcely needs to conceal its imperial aspiration. Finally, the appeal to a colonial heritage outliving its history is recruited to show not only what beneficial service colonizers performed, as committed altruists, but also conscripted as a model for the United States to emulate as it becomes the new imperium of the twenty-first century. But the historical model, as we shall see, was the British Empire, not the French, Japanese, Dutch or even Ottoman.

In this connection, it needs also be said that the category of the "Cold War," so vital for the production of a discourse and discipline called international relations, has constructed a master narrative of struggle between the West and East, "realism" and "idealism" in foreign policy, democracy and communism, recoding in a new register the older polarity between civilization and barbarism, self and other. At the heart of this narrative (still apparently taught as a serious subject in colleges and universities) is the "rise of the West" and all of its claims to unity, fullness, and completion. By the same token, the Cold War master narrative manages to displace and marginalize any agency granted to the Third World, seeking to incorporate it into the First World before the final elimination of the Second, reducing its constituents into shadowy abstractions, the world of the formerly colonized now refitted to becoming "new nations" with American help. But the point to the Cold War narrative was to tell the story of how the U.S. was locked in a life-death struggle to preserve the free world. This meant that its principal aim would be to repress the desire and capacity of these new nations to achieve subjectivity and agency through a third or neutral way different from either first or second worlds, a different politics and economy. In this way the Cold War authorized the United States to continue playing the role of agent of modernization, reinforcing wherever possible the subjectless status of the former colonized by extending aid to "develop" these societies and capitalist markets. At the same time, the United States was willing to use coercion and violence in the form of counter-terrorist espionage, clandestine operations, assassinations (remember Patrice Lumumba?), proxy wars employing terrorists and to risk even full scale war so long as it was outside of Euro-America. For the Soviets it forced greater attempts at integration within their bloc, not always successful as Yugoslavia, Albania, and the Sino-Soviet split of the late 1950s dramatized. Japan became the showcase of the truth of modernization, while India less so because its "democracy" was seen as "unstable," which meant not totally dominated by the United States (in contrast to Japan's single party "democracy") and its leadership too attracted to the lure of neutrality and a different way momentarily promised by the Bandung Conference.

III: PARADIGM'S THEORY

Throughout the decades of the 1960s and 1970s—as we look back today on perhaps the deepest temporal terrain of the Cold War—social science entered the world and acquired its comparative vocation through the formation of a theory of modernization and the construction of a research agenda authorized by its paradigm. Anthropology had already entered the world, so to speak, by leaving its center, and whatever comparative perspective it envisaged was invariably constrained by this location. Disciplines like political science and sociology, especially, which fastened on to developmental programs of decolonizing societies and "new nations" as suitable subject matters for research, often concentrated on the role played by elite leadership and the strategies they employed to negotiate the passage from "tradition" to "modernity." In fact, it is strangely disquieting today to be reminded of the astonishing extent of publications on modernization appearing during this time frame and how seemingly widespread its institutionalization became in education and government. What truly amazes is how so much nonsense could command the time and energies of so many thoughtful people for so long. But arming social science with a global reach and a comparative method invariably meant little more than utilizing some idealized version of American society as its model of replication, a model that scarcely managed to conceal its own exceptionalism and indifference to history. Too often the research agenda was never far from considerations of policy-desire for the formulation of developmental programs promoted by the American state. The trajectory of modernizing development provided a template against which to measure the "progress" or achievement accomplished by a society and what still needed to be done to accelerate or complete the itinerary. The importance of modernization theory, constructed from a neo-evolutionary narrative, lay in its claims to universality, a process of rational achievement that one writer optimistically described as a "universal solvent." In a nutshell the modernizing paradigm's theory rested on a number of "ideal typical" traits: societies were seen as constituted into coherently organized systems whose "subsystems," as the followers of Talcott Parsons called them, were interdependent; societies all followed a scheme of historical development that consisted of the movement (transition?) from tradition to modern that would determine the nature of their social subsystems, with modernity referring to rational, scientific, secular, and Western and tradition signifying the absence of these characteristics and more; and traditional societies, owing to the lack of fullness identified with the completed Self (the West), would resort to the route of modernization—the historical evolution to modernity—with the likelihood of success through resources capable of assisting a process of "adaptive upgrading" (as Jeffrey Alexander calls it).

The Ambition of Post-War Social Science

It should be recognized that modernization theory grew out of two impulses in the post-World War II period. One was the acknowledgement that social theory and the construction of appropriate research agendas confronted an altered environment that demanded accounting for the greater complexity of the globe, especially in view of the consequences of the recent conflict. War's end brought the beginning of a decolonizing process and the appearance of new nation-states in its wake in Africa and Asia; it also produced the need to address the social change such momentous transformations represented and even measure the progress of this ongoing program as it resulted in the proliferation of a number of independent and autonomous societies. The changed intellectual and political landscape required envisaging theories that were able to explain the rates of change and development taking place in an implicitly dynamic, comparative framework. At virtually the same moment a second factor was insinuated into the scene. While decolonization was moving along, the globe was polarized into two contending camps that represented different, competing routes to industrial modernity. With the Soviet Union and its promise of realizing a socialist modernity, Marxism offered both an explanatory strategy that claimed to account for changes over time and the prospect of successful, revolutionary transformation independent of capitalism and its presumed evolutionary trajectory. The United States, as the leading nation of the capitalist world after World War II, and the Soviet Union's principal competitor in the contest to win over the new, recently decolonized, unaligned nations for its path of modernization, promoted political democracy (with a capitalist component, to be sure) as the model of rational modernity, driven by a strategy of evolutionary development. In fact, it was in the immediate post-World War II context that the developmental strategies of both the United States and the Soviet Union were formulated and fine-tuned into explicit state policies leading to the exportation of aid and assistance to new nations; they were directed at "upgrading" the modernizing process and assuring it of rapid success. Modernization, in this respect, became a conception of social change powering the movement of societies from the putatively deadening stand-still of static traditions to the dynamic pace of modernity. By the same measure it was also increasingly perceived by leaders and elites of new nations as a prescriptive policy designated to actualize those changes calculated to achieve the vaunted goal of modernity. This task, more often than not, fell to a group of "Westernized" technocrats more committed to technology than to the blandishments of middle class political democracy. In other words, modernization was envisioned as a policy of planning for transforming "traditional" societies into modern nations by emulating examples of rational achievement and advancement by pressing for, at any cost, the realization of political stability. In this way, it constituted a policy choice initiated by both elites of new nations to complete the decolonizing process and the two, competing world powers which immediately embarked upon promoting their respective, ambitious developmental projects in the ensuing contest. What this demand prompted was a rethinking of social science itself along the lines of fulfilling the desire, read as necessity, to accommodate research to the new, global circumstances.

In the United States until the end of the war, a good deal of social science was weighted down by an approach that sought to emphasize the static countenance of societies and the durable identity of national character or personality derived from repetitive socialization. What plainly was overlooked in the "culture and personality school," as it was called, was, of course, the primacy accorded to the nation form as a framework for social research. The category of nation was presented as an unproblematic presupposition defining the spatial boundary of research (and socialization) as a timeless zone that made no distinction between a past, present, and future. Such an approach was, by nature, unhistorical or even anti-historical and indifferent to change as a significant process. Reflecting, perhaps, unstated claims of American exceptionalism and its own insensitivity to history (a genuine modernist conceit), this approach to social science was incapable of supplying an adequate theory of social change (a necessity already dramatized by war) that could compete with Marxism. Its last, and lasting gasp, was expressed by anthropologists like Ruth Benedict whose *Chrysanthemum and the Sword*

(1947), which, aided by a Nietzschean inspired binary, explained Japanese behavior as a manifestation of an unchanging and endless reproduction of a "shame culture" (as against a Western "guilt culture") and Frances Hsu whose book called *In the Shadow of the Ancestor* managed to make contemporary Chinese identical with their Bronze Age predecessors. Ultimately, the deficiency was filled by structural-functionalism and its willingness to faintly nod toward history and its promise to explain the itinerary of social change from tradition bound past to a modern, advancing present. In time this slight concession to history was compromised when functionalist social science coupled description with prescription in the 1950s and 1960s to meet the demands of policy desire.

But it is, nonetheless, important to recall that even though functionalism initially had shown indifference to historical analysis and comparability, its elevation as America's Cold War social science required acquisition of a methodological strategy no longer constrained by ethnocentric reserve and exceptionalism and sensitive to both history and comparison. The emergence of new nation states necessitated a reassessment of the viability of historico-comparative studies, especially since it concentrated on tracing the passage from tradition to modernity. To meet the challenge posed by the proliferation of new states in different regions of the world, it became essential to acquire an empirical familiarity with different cultures and the status of their current political and economic endowments in order to locate their position in an evolutionary arc. The impulse toward greater comparability would also call for an altering of functionalism's claim to normativity in the study of single societies and contribute to galvanizing a new commitment to conceptions and categories of social change that would permit its generalization. This modification entailed abandoning a modularity founded on an image of American society for one accountable to global diversity, a model specifically addressed to understanding the problems facing emergent nations now implicated in America's future. Moreover, this rehabilitated model would also demand a greater dedication to dynamism for grasping the multiplying complexities of inter-related social processes. But above all else, it would have to deal with the question of conflict. By taking on board neo-evolutionism, functionalist social science, as it morphed into modernization, rarely, if ever, made good on its promise to provide a complex model of society based on a recognition of global diversity. Rather it merely expanded the (idealized) image of America to become the mirror of modernization itself.

The new structural-functionalism behaved similarly to the older approaches to social science, inasmuch as it focused on the interaction of culture and the formation of personality. It proved superior over its predecessor by making up for its principal deficiency—its insensitivity to history—and supplied a processual theory of change. Hence the need for a different kind of social science in the dynamic and ever changing context of the Cold War able to explain development and change and grasp the spectacle of postwar transformations, especially one that might successfully offer a viable alternative to Marxian conflict models and their conception of revolutionary schedule. Structural-functionalism, as this new social science was renamed, and its re-articulation of a social Darwinist program of evolutionary adaptation and development, was thus reconfigured into an export model of growth called modernization and convergence theory. For social science disciplines like political science and sociology, especially, and for a number of historians eager to climb aboard a "scientific" band wagon, it was offered as both a representation of a particular process and an imperative virtually dictated by nature inevitably propelling all societies from the torpor of tradition to a moving modernity. But this appeal to the category of a transition worked only to thinly disguise the older Marxian anxiety over the transformation of feudal into capitalist society and to fulfill its own vocation for embarking upon a prescriptive mission necessitating the implementation of aid and development promising evolutionary growth. In brief, typology was substituted for chronology and Max Weber (plagued by Nietzschean doubts) was transmuted from a nervous, cautious methodologist into the figure of a bold ratifier of empirical reality. If the agenda were followed, it would lead to the promised land of peaceful capitalist development and, presumably, democracy in the world of the new nations. Yet it is important to recognize how modernization theory welded politics to economic growth, often renaming any regime as democratic as long as it seemed empowered to exercise authority in implementing policies leading to "economic take-off." This view was expounded early and consistently by Samuel Huntington, who, during the Vietnam War, apparently favored bombing according to Marilyn Young as inducement for rapid modernization that would compel large scale populations to move from the periphery to the center, that is the cities. The historian Marilyn Young quotes Huntington from an article published in *Foreign Affairs* (1968) that:

> Driving the farmers out of the countryside into refugee camps or cities was seen by some civilian pacification advisers as a "modernizing experience," and by Harvard political scientist Samuel P. Huntington as a legitimate instrument of overall U.S. policy. The Viet Cong, Huntington explained, "is a powerful force which cannot be dislodged from its constituency so long as the constituency continues to exist."

Only force applied "on such a massive scale as to produce a massive migration from countryside to city" could manage to undermine the Maoist inspired rural revolution. For Huntington, the cities constituted the site for political centralization and the necessary precondition for beginning the labor of stabilization.

At the heart of modernization theory, then, was a neo-evolutionary narrative of growth and development that emphasized the centrality of structural differentiation, growing specialization and reintegration, the capacity of societies to buffet change and strains yet reaffirm the essential balance of a social system that has naturally evolved. Adaptation constituted the vehicle of both differentiation and integration, and referred to how units were able to adjust to an environment. The capacity to make adjustments necessitated by environmental changes revealed the mechanism of survival determining the nature of innovation and specialization. As we shall see later in the case of Japan, viewed as the showcase of spectacularly successful modernization outside of Euro-America, this kind of evolutionary adaptation manifest itself when the country made the decision to cast off feudal fetters in the mid-nineteenth century by resituating surviving institutions and values from prior periods at the center of its new, modernizing quest. In this way, the modernization narrative consisted of a linear progression that marked changes in the succession of structures. History constituted a sequence of changes along a progressive developmental grid dividing societies accordingly from the lowest to most advanced levels of achievement.

Within this framework societies were grouped into grades corresponding to their location in the process toward progress and differentiated temporally to reflect their relative maturity in an homogenous continuum of historical time. This arrangement enabled making abstracted comparative judgments that were purely quantitative temporal differences even though they were, in time, translated into qualitative markers, a conception of distancing classically expressed by Hegel in his *Lectures on the Philosophy of History* that has become a staple of social analysis down to the present. The anthropologist Johannes Fabian has described this process as the "radical naturalization of time (i.e. its radical de-historicization)" so central to a comparative method permitting the comprehensive "treatment of human culture at all times and in all places." This belief in natural or evolutionary time enabled classifying past cultures and living societies in a "stream of Time," locating some upstream and others downstream, and plotting all societies and places according to their relative distance from a modern present. But distance always implied velocity and the rate of speed some societies had taken to progress and the time others would need to catch-up. In this comparative scheme some societies were seen to live in another or earlier time. Examples abound in the modernization literature that constantly explain how Third World societies in Africa and Asia lag in some natural temporal spectrum and are not yet modern but traditional and even backward compared to the industrial nations of Euro-America. As a result modernization theory failed singularly to acknowledge that modernity, tradition, past and present were categories of historical totalization in the medium of specific cultural experiences, instead of being mere moments produced by naturalized time. In this way it demanded distinct forms or ways of temporalizing history with which the developmental stages, now identified with lived time, are linked together in the unity of a single, historical view. Societies were ranked then along the continuum to show how they either lagged behind or were poised for achievement, a little like the distinction made earlier by anthropology and Freudian psychoanalysis between childhood and primitive, adulthood and civilized. Some societies were destined never to catch up while others would successfully climb the ladder to reach the top rungs of achievement. Despite the desire of social scientists like Talcott Parsons and S.N. Eisenstadt, principal theorists of modernization, to avoid a singularly linear developmental scheme, they rarely managed to overcome a conceit that set a particular path of progress founded on a Weberian valorization of a specific, Western cultural endowment as normative and exemplary for all societies that pursue the program of modernization. When compared to the Marxian agenda of multiple historical routes to capitalist development, modernization theory risked appearing even more monolithic and politically motivated, even though it scarcely recognized this defect. In fact, it is the very circularity of modernization theory which extracts the modernizing trajectory from a reading of typologies derived from a specific and uniquely West European cultural experience exemplified in its most mature form by the United States that decrees not only the temporality of a unilinear continuum but also a singularly normative model that can only be imitated.

Finally, neo-evolutionary functionalism and its miscreant offspring, modernization theory, placed special emphasis on the role played by culture, both as a motivational force for the development of a specific means/end rationality marking modernity and as the custodian overseeing and sustaining society's customs and rules and its use of power. This task was usually reserved for religion which, again, supplied the surety of ultimate meaning to lived reality and reinforced its claim to normativeness. In this operation, we must

grasp how culture, in its principal religious manifestation, was made to replace capitalism by becoming the
primary agent of social mediation. Religion was
understood to provide the foundation for the subsequent development of socially normative values and
rational behavior. In this way, it supplied the social
system with the principles of legitimacy used to
uphold its view of reality. Moreover, the central role
ascribed to religion in this social configuration was
reinforced by its presumed universality and its claim to
autonomy from society. All of this was harnessed to
an evolutionary trajectory that narrated the natural
unfolding of a process in which culture, especially its
religious practices, ultimately functions to exercise
control over the social structure. Hence, Talcott
Parsons, appropriating the Weberian typology to
make culture perform the labor of social evolution,
once he turned its attention toward history and the
possibility of comparison, simply affirmed the primacy
of the "West" (and behind it the Judeo-Christian religious tradition) in the development of "modernity."
More importantly, Parsons reproduced the divide
between the West and the Rest Max Weber had
already conceptualized in his theory of comparative
religious formations and his typology for a proper
historical sociology. Where Parsons departed from
Weber was in his decision to identify culture and
structure in the evolutionary process and privilege the
former over the latter. It is worth noting that Weber
sought to avoid the prospect of conflict produced by
capitalism by turning to a modernity derived from a
unified and unique religio-cultural endowment that

had evolved over a long duration. He mapped the very divisions he perceived in capitalist society onto a divide between the modern West and the decidedly unmodern Rest. A contemporary of Lenin and witness to emergent social conflict in Europe, Weber constructed a powerful argument that countered and ultimately replaced the Marxian idea of the capitalist mode of production and the revolutionary break it had inaugurated in European life. In Parson's later rereading, his intervention was made to show how the ruptural version of social life and its breach with the past that many had already acknowledged was substituted by the image of a remarkably continuous relationship between capitalism and religion based on their mutual cofiguration. Instead of recognizing the actual fissure generated by capitalism in domestic society, Weber branded the fracture as the difference separating Euro-America from the world outside, proposing that the Chinese and Indian religious traditions may have evolved some form of rationality but one not yet capable of producing capitalist calculation and scientific inquiry. In this way, Weber transmuted the rift between a European past and present into one between the West and the Rest and succeeded along the way in casting out the Rest from history as completely as Hegel had before him. It should be pointed out that Weber saw colonization as a sign of advanced modernity, and Germany's late arrival on the scene looming as a worrisome reminder of insufficient rationality. But it was still an easy step to turn colonies into sites of premodern cultures, whose distance could only be overcome by rejecting an

indigenous heritage and embracing (as he recommended in his famous essay on "objectivity") the
promise of modern, scientific rationality. Modernity,
rather than capitalism (and accumulation), was thus
fixed to a specific place and distinguished by its
distance from the space of the non-modern. The less
developed a society, the more distinct and distant it
appeared from the modular paradigm of modernization employed to structure the relationship to affirm
difference. The concept of late developer, as it was
used widely in modernization studies to describe the
location of societies like Japan, Turkey, China, and
India that apparently had not yet reached full modernity was instantiated by this strategy of distancing and
transfigured what, in fact, was a chronological and
quantitative sign into a qualitative one.

The Moment of Modernization

Following Weber's lead but departing significantly
from his pessimistic outlook, social scientists like
Parsons, Rostow, Bellah, Eisenstadt, Shils, and many
others shaped an optimistic modernization theory that
emphasized the singular importance of the role played
by culture, especially, in the development and divergence of particular geographic and historical experiences (notably, Western Europe) and its distinctive, if
not unique, patterns of rational thought and practice
ultimately figuring the founding of capitalism. Owing
to its peculiar religious foundations, the means/end
rationality would claim for itself normativity and,

more importantly, universal veracity. In the hands of Weber's successors, a generation of American social scientists of the immediate post-World War II period, this normativity was associated with both a description derived principally from a romantic misrecognition of American society and the desire to press for policies that would lead to the replication of the model's exemplars elsewhere in the world. In short, its impulse originated from the push toward producing the convergence of modernization throughout the new and uncommitted nations. With theorists like Parsons, culture was supposed to provide the absolute values governing action. It was also assigned the task of determining the place and character of society's economic and political systems, with law being assigned a primary position in the evolutionary process to modernity.

Anthony Smith has called this narrative "cultural determinism, pure and simple," while others have expanded upon it by distinguishing the emergence of world religions according to an evolutionary scheme (Bellah) and their progressive differentiation which, in the Judeo-Christian tradition, not surprisingly, have managed to sharpen the distance between the self and the outside world and ultimately provide the sanction for change. S.N. Eisenstadt, perhaps the long distance runner of modernization studies, locates this great divergence in the formation of the world's religions in archaic times, designating their "axiality" (the term is from Karl Jaspers) in order to signal the moment of emergence of coherent civilizations between 500 BCE and the first century of the common era, along with the production of conflict between other worldly and worldly orders and their institutionalization. For Eisenstadt, axiality, identified with the world's salvation religions, furnished a basis for broad, historical comparability, in keeping with both functionalism's and modernization theory's penchant for large scale structural analyses as a prior condition for micro-studies. But behind this elaborate historical sociology still lurks the Weberian identification of a unique religio-cultural endowment capable of generating a means/end rationality based on normative (universal) values. What Eisenstadt has turned to in his later work is the problem of explaining why Japan represents the one non-axial civilization that has managed to become modern on its own. On his part, Robert Bellah had earlier explained Japan's meteoric success as a modernizer because of the presence of an analogue to the Protestant ethic in its own religious tradition that could function as a motivational motor.

Too often in this vast literature there has been the easy bonding between forms of rationalization conceived by Weber, which remain culturally specific, and the process of differentiation and specialization as advanced by Parsons and his many followers. Where this tactic falters is in (1) its willingness to presume that "empirical" and "historical" certainty equal methodological typologizations and (2) its misrecognition of Weber's interpretation of rationalization as an outgrowth of a specific religio-cultural configuration which, by being made to function as the West's unique difference from the rest of the world, became the sign of its crowning achievement and claim to universality.

Unlike Weber, Parsons and his followers saw in the pattern of social evolution leading to the development of modern Western societies the culmination of a beneficial historical process. Differentiation meant purposive movement directed toward the accomplishment of the "universalistic-achievement pattern" which characterizes advanced industrial societies like the United States. By contrast, less differentiated societies will know only "primitive diffuseness" and an absence of any real distinction between cultural, political, and economic domains. While Weber offered a gloomy forecast of the consequences of rationalization (differentiation), Parsons, and especially modernization theory, reworked it into an upbeat and optimistic narrative leading to new patterns of stratification, new forms of egalitarianism, associationism, liberal and plural democracies that impede illegitimate concentrations of power and bring an end to the tyranny of ascription based on status. In the early 1950s, he was already convinced that this "trend toward modernization has now become worldwide."

In any case, it is important to recognize how this extraordinary partiality for cultural categories has been ceaselessly deployed (well beyond the moment of modernization) to explain either the absence of social change (differentiation) or its presence as a response to what was seen as Marxism's emphasis on material (economic) forces motoring transformation. In the world of the 1950s and 1960s these two positions were enacted by the United States and the Soviet Union on a global stage to produce a conflict which immediately authorized a binary strategy inscribed in social science.

What seems so remarkable now, as we look back on this almost forgotten and frequently unreadable literature on modernization, is not just simply its commitment to a logic of abstraction and generalization that worked to conceal its indifference to historical specificity and the details of the contemporary conjuncture, its obsession with molar over molecular analysis, but also its elaborate effort to mask the very materiality represented by capitalism informing its own theory of modernity, social change, and development. Where Weber saw a complex, ideal-typical interweaving of religion and capitalism, his successors actually simplified it by identifying the model with historical reality and flattened out the causal chain by replacing capitalism with culture. By appealing to the empowerment of cultural practice and spiritual values as principal determinants of structure and their subsequent "differentiation," modernizers were permitted to employ social Darwinist sign-posts attesting to the survival of traditional values and institutions whose endurance now qualified them to play the new role as mediators in the transition to modernity. The continued existence of traditional residues and their redeployment as mediators of modernization testifies to the power of the neo-evolutionary narrative to unfold peaceably and utilize what was near at hand in its progress to the next stage of achievement. In this scenario, the question of history was always bracketed since its importance diminished in contrast to the movement of deeper patterns, the ceaselessly continuous process of adaptation that eventually, like a huge geologic formation, would aggregate into structural change. The indifference to history, as such, sprung from a dismissal of events, to be sure, which invariably were classified as external, ephemeral (and discontinuous), and unenduring. Marion Levy, a sociologist who wrote one of the first modernization tracts on the Chinese family, attributed the occurrence of change to forces endogenous to the family itself—how it, as a social unit, managed strains and tensions, in the words of Smith, "created by, but continued within, the 'traditional' structure." One wonders what happened to the war with Japan that raged through China in the 1930s and early 1940s and the momentous Chinese revolution, which was about to explode precisely the moment the book was being published.

In this way, modernization upheld the primacy of culture and its values; as the source of value (rather than labor), it came to replace the commodity form as the "germinal cell" and agent that structured society. For many of its proponents the process was comprehended as a ceaseless human quest to accumulate greater knowledge in order to better master nature. Others specified the centrality of "learning to learn" (Bellah) and the talent for following directions (R.P. Dore). Ever the devoted Weberian, Eisenstadt envisaged the operation of rational understanding as the necessary condition of society's propensity for producing change and incorporating it. Throughout the literature there was a remarkably uniform commitment to the importance of maintaining a balance between the mechanisms of structural change (differentiation) and continuity with a traditional inheritance. (One can almost see the sociologist Edward

Shils, a principal theorist of the concept of traditionalism, playing the role of Tevye in *Fiddler on the Roof*,
and belting out a chorus of the song, "TRADITION!,"
but perhaps not as robustly as Zero Mostel.) Here, in
any case, the line dividing description from prescription was blurred since in modernization texts it was
never clear if local elites of new nations were pursuing
this exemplar or it was pursuing them through policy
formation and developmental programs initiated by
advanced societies. But the heavy reliance on the part
played by persisting cultural values in the modernization process constantly demanded the adaptation of
older practices and values to new circumstances and
their evolutionary mutation as society confronts the
challenge posed by the industrial West, its modern
environment, and successfully overcomes the threat
posed to continuing survival by emulating the chal-
lenger.

With the apparent introduction of an external
or "exogenous" challenge (one thinks of its use in
Arnold Toynbee's popular and more bought than read
A Study of History of the early 1950s and J.K.
Fairbank's emplotment of China's modern history as a
"response to the West") societies were forced with the
choice of either drawing upon received resources to
figure an adaptive response, invariably entailing
greater differentiation, or falling prey to the alien
dictates of total revolutionary transformation. In
effect the appeal to an adaptive tradition required the
usual autonomization of spheres ("subsystems")
induced by the introduction of and incorporation into
a new mode of production and its concomitant scien-

tific, technological, organizational and financial requirements. To be sure, the process of modernization, when driven by a decision to maintain an equilibrium between "continuity" and "change" or an impulse toward ever greater differentiation and specialization necessitated by successive re-integration will, as the story line goes, produce powerful strains and unscheduled disturbances, violent disruptions threatening to undermine the loose stability of the changing social edifice. It was precisely the function of deploying re-integrative mechanisms (all inspired by Durkheim's idea of the "division of labor" and his later conceptualization of the evolution of "elementary religious forms") that would head off possible conflict and diminish the spread of anomic violence. But as Neil Smelser showed, greater or increased utilization creates the need for even more differentiation, as in an endless game resembling musical chairs but producing constant "asymmetries." Caught in this circular movement of differentiation and integration, it is as difficult to determine when modernization will have completed its evolutionary itinerary as it is to know how many swallows make a summer. What is so striking in this narrative is its similarity to a Marxian analysis of how the reproduction of capitalist accumulation is motored by a principle that can only produce unevenness within all levels of the social formation, an operation that signifies how capitalism itself is nothing if it is not the law of uneven and unequal development. Yet in the modernization narrative only the form of unevenness is recuperated, not its content which is capital accumulation. While social scientists like Smelser have acknowledged the Trotskyean *locus classicus* of the idea of unevenness it is less clear whether their appropriation of its form as expressed in categories like "differentiation" and "integration" has improved upon its original Marxian meaning.

A final consideration of this discourse worth mentioning is the crucial role played by "native elites" and their dependence upon "external" sources of training and outside resources in order to carry out the modernizing project. Even though this inflection of modernization appeared in the writings of Edward Shils, who attributed great importance to the formation of native elites occupying the "center" they would articulate with a periphery (recognizing once more a paradigmatic instance of unevenness between city and countryside perceived by Marx without actually acknowledging it), it was Eisenstadt who made the most of the relationship. Even Wallerstein, despite his critique of the social science propagating modernization theory and his recommendation calling for a return to considering the role of capitalism, recuperated the structural dyad of center and periphery to divide the world's economic domains. Eisenstadt, in any case, envisaged a direct link between the development of native elites and their acquisition of knowledge, skills, expertise and aspiration for change from contact with missionaries and colonial administrations. The significance of this observation, shared widely throughout the literature, is that it transferred the emphasis on internal and endogenously motivated change to the outside, as it were, to the agency of external forces that supply both the opportunity for training native elites, providing models, ideas, and access to material resources. Eisenstadt also accounted for developmental lags in the comparative process but recognized the singular significance of the difference between late comers like new nations and early modernizers. The difference signaled the "advantages of backwardness," effectively repressing the destructive consequences of colonial expropriation and violence, to make adversity into a blessing. Late comers were thus in the happy position to learn from the experience of early achievers—their forbearers—and, more importantly, to take advantage of mistakes that would short circuit the modernizing process and speed up the evolutionary pace. Inserting elite groups in the process as mediators resulted in reconfiguring an essentially static model of modernization driven by the anonymous force of evolution for one that now was moved by identifiable agents who were making history. Although the commitment to create a pool of native experts, managers, and administrators situated to oversee the process raises more questions than it can possibly answer (reflecting, too, an earlier conceit that valorized the "floating intellectual" and un-classed scientific experts—not for nothing did Shils translate Karl Mannheim), one of its most baneful consequences was to connect the modernizing process among new nations to patron states, an external agency, that risked transforming the postcolony into a neo-colonial site. Amilcar Cabral put it best long ago when he described this process as historical theft:

> The colonialists usually say that it was they who
> brought us into history: today we show that this is
> not so. They made us leave history, our history, to
> follow them, right at the back, to follow the
> progress of their history.

Modernization theory's paradigm, in short, was opened
up to the agency of external intervention which, in the
Cold War world of the 1960s and 1970s, meant inviting from the outside the active intervention of aid and
development programs targeting the unaligned.

     Yet it must also be conceded that social scien-
tists in the 1970s, especially from political science,
were convinced that these "Westernized" bureaucratic
and technocratic elites would constitute an urban
middle stratum and act thus as firm foundation for the
formation of democracy in the new nations. The argument, as it had been developed by people like Shils and
Eisenstadt, proposed that these social groups, educated
and occupying privileged social status, would be positioned to play a commanding role in the political life of
the developing society. Accordingly, social science
endowed in this elite the possibility for playing a
"providential" role throughout the Third World,
supplying both technical and bureaucratic expertise
and the crucial backing for the subsequent democratization of their societies, the continuation and stabilization of national institutions and the "successive transformation of the social structure." But despite their
impressive qualifications the very group who W.W.
Rostow identified were in the position to expect assistance and resources from industrial democracies, as

observed by B. Kagarlitsky, proved to be the "grave-
diggers" of political freedom and modernization rather
than its "guardians." It is interesting to note that even
in the much heralded example of Japan's political
modernization, the democratization so prominently
advertised as the American military occupation's greatest, lasting achievement, was ultimately forfeited to
the requirements of bureaucratic and technical expertise, symbolized by "single party rule." In time, social
science came around to this view that dismissed the
accomplishment of democratization, perceiving it as
an obstacle in the process of political modernization,
for other, often coercive forms that promised both the
prospect of stability and the chance for unimpeded
development.

Modernization's Holy Trinity: Economic, Political, and Social

In its developmental modality, modernization theory
concentrated on explaining ways of achieving
economic growth, principally the expansion of capitalism (Rostow) and the necessary political conditions—
what we might call the political form—that would
enable far-reaching economic change (Huntington).
Both Rostow's *The Stages of Economic Growth* and
Huntington's *Political Order in Changing Societies*
appeared in the early 1960s, during the decade of the
Vietnam War and the time of developmentalism's
most intense maturation, what, in fact, had once been
called the "decade of development." In the late 1950s

Rostow, an economic historian who served as an advisor to President Lyndon Johnson during the Vietnam War, published *The Stages of Economic Growth*, which he subtitled "A Non-Communist Manifesto." The work underwent innumerable printings and was widely seen as a template for economic growth among the world's unaligned nations. Its purpose was to propose an elaborate theory of economic development through the tracing of a series of sequentially progressive stages of evolutionary growth which, if followed, promised success. While Rostow envisioned a blueprint for economic growth as an alternative to Soviet Communism, he was actually referring to capitalism, even though he imagined his successive stages as an "industrializing process" in a comparative global context exemplifying the course of development that sought to take the study beyond the Soviet case. In fact, it would now be accurate to say that Rostow's program presciently prefigured a contemporary impulse toward what today is called "globalization," inasmuch as his developmental program prescribed precise stages a nation must pass through in order to sustain the "drive to maturity" and enter the "age of High mass consumption." Undoubtedly, Rostow's conceptualization grew out of his own acknowledged antipathy for "Marxism-Leninism" and his dim estimate of the accomplishments of the Soviet economy. No hesitation inhibited him from envisioning the "affluent suburbs" of the United States, which he contrasted with communism, as the model for global integration under the full development of a capitalist system.

Like most modernizing enthusiasts of the time, Rostow placed great emphasis upon the significance of the category of "traditional society" (based on "pre-Newtonian science" and attitudes) and the constraints it imposed on output. The whole of the pre-Newtonian world consisted of dynastic China, the civilizations of the Middle East and the Mediterranean, and Medieval Europe. Social orders evolved into a second stage of growth in societies in the process of transition, which meant simply the time when the "pre-conditions" for "take-off" are developed. In Rostow's reckoning, Western Europe led the way. But he was also convinced that the normal route to modernization reflected the force of outside intervention "by more advanced societies" in the undoing of a traditional order. Such shocks undermined the failing order to "set into motion ideas and sentiments" capable of initiating modern alternatives. An essential element in this equation was the appearance of local elites committed to organizing what Rostow called "strong, modern political structures prepared to take on the task of building an industrial society." The transition stage is succeeded by what Rostow famously called "take-off," now navigated by a new leadership that has managed to overcome the received obstacles to growth and become identified with "the force making for economic progress," as growth itself becomes the normal condition of society. "Compound interest becomes built, as it were, into its habits and institutional structure." After successful "take-off," Rostow was convinced, the growing economy enters the long internal development leading to maturity, usually marked by the extension of modern technology along the wide front of economic activity. The utopian moment, presumably when real history begins, is announced by the age of high mass consumption (what Marx earlier referred to as the completion of the commodity relation). At this juncture, there is an apparent epochal shift toward the production of durable consumer goods and services, a stage already reached by the United States, with West Europe and Japan closing in and the Soviet Union still engaged in an "uneasy flirtation." We must recognize here that Rostow's "age of high consumption" was the inspiration for Prime Minister Ohira Masayoshi's 1970s plan called the "age of culture," which Japanese would soon experience: mass consumption and garden cities everywhere. Leaving nothing to historical chance, Rostow was quick to cement the relationship between cooperative native elites (a vestige of colonialism) and developmental help from advanced nations. These leaders, he writes, "have the right to expect the world of advanced democracies to help on an enlarged scale." But it is they "who having achieved independence under the banners of human freedom, appealing to those values in the West which they share, must now accept... the responsibility for making those values come to life." They also would constitute the core of the affluent minorities who benefit most from marketization.

If Rostow looked to the agency of local elites who shared Western values as the group best poised to inaugurate modernizing changes and receive developmental assistance, he was plainly pointing to the formation of a "middle class" committed to democracy. By contrast, the work on political modernization from the 1950s on, carried on by a virtual army of political scientists like Almond and Coleman, Apter, LaPalombara, and others too numerous to mention (who was actually reading this mountain of literature is the question that needs to be answered) the views of Huntington probably best exemplify the strange convergence between "realism" and "rationality." For Huntington, and most political scientists working in the modernizing idiom, what mattered most for the modernizing process was less the availability of a fully formed middle class, prepared to undertake the traditional role of bringing about a bourgeois revolution, and who shared Western values and were devoted to democratic practice, as such, than it was the existence of a coherent leadership competent to put into play the necessary institutional programs and to secure the goal of political stabilization. Like so many adherents of modernization theory in the 1960s and 1970s, Huntington was less interested in the achievement of modern society as in the example of a democratic order than in forestalling and eliminating the specter (or spectacle) of disorder found in traditional societies. In his influential *Political Order in Changing Societies* (1968) he early acknowledged that his purpose resembles those who purport to deal with "economic development: whose actual subjects are economic backwardness and stagnation." Recalling the example of developmental economists who invariably favor the realization of the "industrial process," his concern was intended to grasp in societies embarked upon disruptive modernizing changes the challenge of how to achieve a measure of political stability to contain the excess. Huntington explicitly de-linked social modernization—"democracy, stability, structural differentiation, achievement patterns, national integration from political modernization"—and warned against the temptation to "ascribe to a political system qualities which are assumed to be its ultimate goals rather [than those] which actually characterize its processes and functions." In other words, the primary importance of a regime was to secure the semblance of political order, opening the door to virtually any kind of political control so long as it could demonstrate its success in stabilizing society. Democracy would come later. Often, the modernizing process undermined trends toward competitiveness and democracy, causing "an erosion of democracy," and showing a propensity for military regimes and one-party governments. Moreover, stability was frequently by-passed for a steady stream of revolts, coups and rebellions to suggest only that political modernization in developing countries meant simply mobilization and participation, beyond the village level, by social groups throughout society and the formation of newer political organizations to further it. Despite Huntington's willingness to accept the agency of traditional political elites and practices in mediating the process of political modernization, he more often than not recognized how these received endowments constituted impediments to change and how their hostility to innovation required strenuous forms of adaptation and incorporation that invited greater instability. But the change from "traditional man" to "modern man" involved "a fundamental psychological shift in values, attitudes and expectations." This transformation consisted of a quantum leap from particularistic loyalties and identifications with family, clan, and village to the broader world of impersonal relationships, like class and nation, and the ultimate "reliance on universalistic...value" and achievement rather than ascription. Such a world closely resembled the image of a Euro-American rational, capitalistic society he would later identify in the figure of a unified Western Civilization that would stand and defend the gates against the encroachments of precisely those (barbarian?) societies that had failed the test of realizing political stability.

In this regard, Huntington already pointed to the appearance of a "mobile personality" (the phrase quoted from Daniel Lerner's "classic" *The Passing of Traditional Society* of 1958) that sociologists like Alex Inkeles and David Smith would seek to locate in a massive survey of six developing countries in order to nail down the "individual common man" who has "become modern." Inkeles and Smith sought to supply substance to an "ideal type" through the massive machinery of questionnaires to operationalize what they confidently called "Overall Modernity Scales" (OMS). "Our results" they concluded, "provide definitive evidence that living individuals do indeed conform to our model of the modern man...." If ever an act of representation failed the test of referentiality this was it. The informed participant observer was possessed of what they called a "marked sense of personal efficacy: highly independent and autonomous in his relations to traditional sources of influence" in his personal conduct, and prepared for "new experiences and ideas," open ended and "cognitively flexible." Inkeles and Smith boasted that they had given reality to an ideal type which others like Marx, Weber, Robert Redfield, David Reisman, and E.V. Stonequist had only approximated.

Fueled by a powerful evolutionary narrative devoted to demonstrating how societies are able to overcome disorder and achieve stability for growth, modernization theory, what Wallerstein in the 1970s called "world social science," became the favored social theory of choice for both scholarly analysis of the emerging new nations and the driving force propelling the formation and implementation of ambitions programs of aid and assisted development. What gave its paradigm of growth and stabilization the aura of authority was, of course, the status of postwar American society which, as so few other societies, had reached the exalted level of achievement and would thus constitute an "empirical" model for others to follow. Not too many years ago, Jeffrey Alexander tried to explain the enthusiastic embracing of this paradigm by referring to a postwar context which, far from celebrating its luminous promise, saw modernization theory as both a realist dismissal of the heady optimism of the prewar and a downgrading of expectations, what he described as a deflation. But this assessment is, I suspect, an effort to defend social science against earlier attacks that condemned modernization as a *cul de sac* and for its total devaluation derived from a cozy relationship with the Vietnam War, along with more contemporary expressions that point to its service to imperial ambitions. What Alexander has described as "deflation," an end to the prewar innocence of American social science epitomized in Daniel Bell's premature conclusion announcing the end of ideology, actually signified a rather smug satisfaction, buoyed by an optimism inspired by the prospects of postwar American society's achievement, presaging a glorious future and what the accomplishment offered to the coming new age of global convergence and integration. Alexander, it seems, is able to defend modernization theory as a viable social science in this way only by isolating it from both the world it sought to refigure in countless studies (the object to its subjective privilege) and the state that made this figuration the principle of developmental policies. Nowhere was this optimistic faith more repetitiously enunciated than in all those studies that sought to show the empirical reality of successful cases of modernization.

IV: PRACTICING THE PARADIGM

It was this abiding faith in the desirability and necessity of reconfiguring the world according to a normative model that motored both social science as it entered the world in the appearance of modernization theory and the state devoted to promoting its promise. Development was thus designed to account for America's entry into the global economy and fulfill the wish to realize a stable environment for capitalist expansion, exactly the concern that prompted modernization theorists and proponents to worry about the incidence of disorder found in traditional societies and recommend a model of emulation claiming stability. In the ensuing Cold War, the contest was cloaked as a competition between two basically different economic systems promising development. But each barely avoided betraying its informing imperial interest. Only with the collapse of the Berlin Wall and the end of actually existing socialism was it possible for the United States to shed the altruistic moralism masking modernization and development for more direct strategies leading to unilateral and pre-emptive (not even remotely preventative) military occupation, conquest, and occupation. The purpose of imperial intervention is regime change, in today's idiom, imposing order on unstable polities. The concern for development was always to over-ride local sovereignties in the interest of establishing political order for the accomplishment of a higher principle. Yet it is because of this aspiration that the echoes of early modernizing policies to stem traditional disorder are still audible in this imperial project. The goal today, as it was then, is to reconfigure the globe in such a way as to remove precisely those forces of destabilization that threaten the expansion of American capital.

The Cold War's Three Worlds

Social science crudely divided the postwar world into a three tiered classification composed of first, second and third worlds. The tripartite scheme represented a response to the exigencies of the Cold War and constituted what Carl Pletsch has called "three conceptual worlds" that had a major impact on the "allocation of social scientific division of labor" that has come down from the 1950s and 1960s to our present day. The division was early incorporated into social science practice as if it were a category dictated by nature and has continued to serve as the lens through which to differentiate the spheres of the globe according to their proximate relationship to modernity. In more recent years, the north-south classification has entered into the mix to lend more precision to the organization of the contemporary world and to delineate greater definition to the task of achieving global integration in the post Cold War era. For most social scientists, the Second World, now a fading silhouette, which once was seen to occupy the place of the polar opposite to the First World, was invariably by-passed for the Third World, the sublime object of desire of the Cold War struggle. But the category of Third World was simply a renaming of "backwardness," the "underdeveloped," and even "non-West" conveying both negativity and traces of more distant classifications like "primitive," "uncivilized," and "savage." Underlying its concept was the older binary authorizing the division between West and East, modern and traditional which, as we've already seen, was employed by modernization theory to equip its analysis with a comparative and evaluative perspective. All of these associations, and probably more, were covered by the encompassing umbrella provided by the term tradition, whose invocation literally reverberated with images of the teeming masses of Asia and Africa and the great "unwashed." Although the category of the Third World circulated throughout social science practice and area studies programs, its attractiveness was eclipsed by favoring other terms that seemed to speak more directly of the current situation in the world beyond Euro-America, like "underdeveloped," "new nations," and "non-Western" (note the negativity) which often would include the Soviet Union and its bloc, in policy considerations and academic agendas in the non-communist societies. War's end, in any case, had seen the emergence of Soviet power (the first area studies programs at Harvard and Columbia were devoted to Russian studies and already linked to the state and policy-making) and steady decolonization of the British, French, and Dutch empires and the transfer of responsibility to new nations created in the wake.

Area studies was formulated in this context principally to supply the national security state (erected by the Truman administration) with a fund of reliable knowledge of formerly colonized regions or of those, like China, that had known semi-colonial status, now on their way to becoming independent nation states. Hence, modernization theory afforded the channel through which social science entered the wider world and the means by which area studies was opened to social science. But it is important to recognize, here, that modernization became the singular vocation of area studies, its theory, so to speak, its principal *raison d'etre* guiding its choice of what to appropriate from social science. This peculiar triangulation between social science, modernization theory, and area studies programs in the U.S. goes a long way to explaining why so much research was carried out on developing societies and the role this research played in the formation of policy and the implementation of developmental programs. In this respect, it was often difficult to differentiate between these three points of the scholarly compass from policies dedicated to development. As modernization became an American imperative for the Third World, research agendas and training centers devoted to the holistic study of discrete regions of the world (South Asia, Africa, Latin America, East Asia) proliferated and quickened the search for identifying the institutional, political, social, and especially, cultural conditions best suited for successful development. Pletsch had argued in the early 1980s for the unavoidable bonding of modernization theory and the classification of the three worlds, at the moment when its interpretative force had already been dismissed. But this was, perhaps, a premature forecast. Because modernization theory relied on a

neo-evolutionary scheme, its authorization of developmental stages lighting up the golden road to modernity, an alchemy that transmuted the lesser metal of
tradition into the precious alloy of modernity (a fool's
gold, if there ever was one) revealed a "salvationist"
mission reflecting an earlier enlightenment seculariza-
tion of progress, bringing together the heavenly city on
earth, Hegel's end of history, and Parsons' sign of
"election."

If, moreover, area studies and modernization
formed a fatal alliance, its principal condition of effectivity demanded ignoring or overlooking or even
displacing considerations of colonialism which had
characterized the historical experience of so many
societies that had recently been re-classified as non-
Western and underdeveloped. It was one of the unfulfilled recommendations of Edward Said's critique of
the epistemological and discursive scaffolding of colonial power (*Orientalism*) that the practice of area studies in American colleges and universities incorporate
into its research and teaching programs the role
played by colonialism and imperialism. Instead, as we
shall see, this particular assignment unfortunately
migrated to departments of English and cultural studies, while area studies remained chained to the
modernization paradigm and stubbornly mired in the
politics of Cold War developmentalism and capitalist
integration on a global scale. I will return to this
theme below.

In the pit of the Cold War, liberal social
science scholarship turned to producing a staggering
array of research on diverse areas of the world, all seen

to be occupying, to a greater or lesser extent, one of Rostow's early stages for "take-off." Although much of this literature concentrated on the poorer regions of the globe (but even France and Italy in the 1950s underwent a modernizing process) it singled out for special attention three non-Western societies to show how different strategies produced results that might be employed as positive and negative models in the contest for the uncommitted. All three of these societies were Asian: India, Communist China, and Japan. The first two were marked by a colonial and semi-colonial historical past, the third by a successfully rapid but late response to the challenge of modernization which momentarily was derailed into fascism and an imperialist war but was returned to its proper path by an American army of occupation. China had failed to make the proper adaptive response to its environment and had fallen prey to communist revolution. India was upheld as an example of a fragile democratic order, and its colonial heritage was implicated in this plot line only to show beneficial contributions the British had made to subsequent modernization. Until, that is, post-colonial discourse and subaltern historiography emerged to settle the score with the past. Even Barrington Moore, a pointed critic of Parsonian social science and its theory of modernization, saw India's response to modernization undermined by obstacles prior to the British conquest, whose colonial structure simply took over the previous Mughal administration, inadvertently recuperating the historiographical narrative of the Cambridge School. Moreover, Moore attributed failed or compromised modernization to other factors that appeared later as a result of Britain's imperial seizure. Specifically, Moore argued that the "foreign conqueror" (both Mughal and British), the landlord, and the money lender absorbed the surplus produced by the country's vast peasantry. Colonial India embarked upon its path of economic stagnation begun with the Mughals and has continued down to the present. Yet the British, Moore wrote, "prevented the formation of the characteristic reactionary coalition of landed elites with a weak bureaucracy" (presumably found in fascist Japan and Germany), and thus opened the way for the development of political democracy which was institutionalized after decolonization. But it remained weak, according to most modernization analysts and unstable because of its failure to modernize the social system.

Moore, perhaps unintentionally, played down the more repressive features of colonial rule for its lasting political legacy that acknowledged its contribution of political democracy to the later Indian state. More importantly, he overlooked the obvious fact that India, already linked to the Bandung Conference and the hope for a neutralist, third way, failed to conform to American expectations of economic and political modernization. In this regard Japan, as we shall see, was the ideal model precisely because it had become an American colony and client state, complete with a permanent army of occupation. With China, the abject failure of the Chinese nationalists to alter elite control and life at the local level, and the continuation of a pervasive landlordism gave the communists the opportunity to mobilize an immense peasant constituency removed from the direct control of the rulership to break the bonds between landed property and kinship, as well as village structure, to foment powerful class antagonism. But as a strategy for successful modernization (which for Moore meant democratization) China, even more so than Russia, found in the peasantry the principal driving force for victory of the party devoted to achievement through "relentless terror." It was thus the perceived threat of violence and terror that would rule the Chinese example and underscore the attractiveness of the Japanese achievement, despite its recent brush with state fascism and imperial war.

In the 1960s and 1970s the Japanese example, which Moore rightly tried to diminish by calling attention to its unflattering fascist interlude, the apparent curse of late developers, became the show-case of modernization. (By the time Moore's book was published the memory of Japan's fascist interlude had been virtually effaced by enthusiastic supporters of modernization.) The upshot of Moore's study was to provide a comparative framework for historical modernization that would concentrate more on social and economic patterns than the conduct of normative values. But his historical sociology contributed more to reaffirming precisely those routes (the U.S., U.K., France) that had evolved earlier into viable political democracies. In the historical configuration of the 1960s, when the book appeared, this liberal critique worked simply to reinforce the theory of moderniza-tion social science was already plying by demonstrat-ing which paths best offered the promise of realizing a successful political democracy and which strategies would actually stunt, delay, and divert proper growth. Along the way, Moore also unintentionally provided a powerful boost to later theorization committed to emphasizing not the baleful influence of colonialism and the nemesis of its lingering legacy on new nations but rather its contributions to subsequent political and economic modernization of the postcolony. On the basis of his logic, a logic carried to extremes by recent enthusiasts of a new imperialism, Japan would have been better off had it been colonized by Great Britain.

America's *Island of Dr. Moreau*

Notwithstanding Moore's stern judgement concerning Japan's historical experience and its "dysfunctional" route to modernization, Cold War America actually validated the Japanese example as a model of peaceful, evolutionary modernization. In fact, Japan's experience was seen as so successful that its prewar fascism, imperialism, and colonialism were soon forgotten (deliberately effaced is more accurate) and written off as a momentary and episodic departure from its true course. This particular removal of the memory of fascism was particularly necessary to make the model appear as unblemished and, later, even useable for developmentally prone historians and social scientists who looked to colonialism as a primary agency in the subsequent modernization of former colonies like Korea and Taiwan. For the United States, Japan would thus justify the military occupation and its ambitious attempt to transform its society to play a crucially strategic role in the Cold War contest under the sign of successful, non-revolutionary modernization by a "non-Western" nation. In a certain sense, an historical irony flared up in this re-figuration that threatened to repeat in a different register a role assigned to Japan during the Russo-Japanese war of 1904-05, when the country became the object of veneration of all those Asians aspiring to rid their societies of white man's colonialism as a condition of securing national independence. Then, a half century later, the unaligned were invited to emulate the Japanese experience of modernization, presumably without going through the tumult of its fascist agony. But the difference, not always concealed, was that the United States utilized Japan (with Japanese complicity, to be sure) as a mask, a "beard," to promote a conception of modernization more American and imperial than Japanese, even though Japan's success was frequently attributed to a uniquely irreducible cultural endowment. On one brief occasion, Japan was even elevated to a level of superiority over its American sponsor, and momentarily was renamed "Japan as number one."

There are two, mutually related, dimensions that went into making Japan the showcase of modernization in the Cold War era: active involvement of an American military occupation between 1945-1952 and its continuation since that time under the provisions of the U.S.-Japan Security Pact, and the recoding of Japan's modern history into an instance of modernization in scholarly social science writing in the 1960s and 1970s, especially, and early 1980s. In fact, the military occupation interlude was fused with the modernization narrative so effectively that it would become the historical analogy of choice when the U.S. invaded Iraq. In no time at all, Japan, a former foe, was transmuted into friend but not full-fledged partner, an autonomous nation into a dependent client of a newly emerging, postwar imperium.

The American military occupation of Japan was directed by General Douglas MacArthur, Supreme Commander of the Allied Powers from 1945 to 1952, who shamelessly enacted the role of a Roman proconsul lacking only a toga and sandals, ruling the country as a distant colony of a vast empire. (Neither the feckless ex-general Jay Garner nor Paul Bremer III in Iraq come even close to replicating MacArthur's larger than life *figura*.) The American occupation departed from other, historic examples of imperial colonization in deciding early on to "remake" the Japanese and their society, what today has been renamed "regime change." The occupation of Japan signaled the end of a long, murderous war in the Pacific and the Asian mainland stretching back to 1931, one that, at the ideological level, Japan fought to rid the country of an "Americanism" already actively implicated in the reshaping of culture and society. It also announced the defeat of a fascist regime aligned with Hitler and Mussolini in what might have been the paradigmatic axis of evil. While a war-weary population in Japan failed to greet the coming of American troops, or dance jubilantly in the streets, it offered no resistance. The Americans, rather than merely fulfilling an obligation to protect the defeated country from itself, sought immediately to remake it into a functioning democracy, supported by a social and economic base composed of small, business capitalists (reinforced by land reforms that broke up large estates to create a class of petit bourgeois farmers, still the principal base of Japan's single party hegemony led by the Liberal-Democrats).

Once recognized that Japan would have to occupy the larger role scripted for it as America's leading ally in East Asia, owing to the immanent collapse of the Chinese nationalist regime, planners and administrators would discover their model of transformation in the image of small town American society (romanticized by Parsonianism). Although this re-narrativizing of Japan by the American military would become the central plot-line of social science at a later time, as we shall see, reshaped through the mediation of modernization theory, it was the opening shot in the Cold War struggle to preserve the normative values of the free world and prevent the spread of communist revolution by promoting development aimed at installing a putative "universal/rational ethos" against the forces of politically deformed particularisms, scheduled, peaceful transformation over the threat of upheaval. In this respect, modernization was simply a mutation of an imperialism and colonialism discredited by World War II, not because of any general agreement that they had represented domination, exploitation, and violent oppression but rather because of the alibi that they were no longer, if ever, profitable. The American military occupation of Japan, and its subsequent inflections in countless social scientific studies devoted to exemplifying the "experience," combined to mark the place of a new stage of imperialism and colonialism without overt territorial ambition. But this never meant a complete foreswearing of territorial aspirations, since through the framework of a joint U.S.-Japan Security Pact, the United States acquired a number of military and naval bases it has retained since the end of the war.

Under the sanction of this new charge, Occupation authorities envisaged Japan as a vast, social and political laboratory, dedicated to "experiments" that would lead to changing and altering the deepest behavioral and institutional patterns of society. These experiments, probably unprecedented in the annals of empire, often recalled those performed by the cruel, mad but "masterful physiologist" Dr. Moreau, on his island laboratory, but on a scale never imagined in H.G. Wells' novel. Through a series of political, economic, educational, and social reforms, carried out in record breaking time, the American authorities were convinced that Japanese could be changed from Benedict's conformist, shame-ridden population into a democratic (and petit bourgeois) citizenry competent to make responsible and informed decisions in their own, newly found interest. But the very subjectivity the occupation reforms sought to invest in the Japanese was effectively cancelled out by the way they—the reforms—were implemented and imposed on a subjected population as if they were objects to be worked on. It is entirely possible that this tactic of supplying subjectivity by effectively nullifying it through imposed programs premised on the necessity of maintaining the hierarchy of a subject-object relation, worked out first in Japan, became the operational principle of modernization theory. In any case, its retention conformed to the hierarchical social structure of imperial design that still defines America's relationship to the world outside of Euro-America.

Yet the occupation's "experiments" uncannily recalled Moreau's failure to mold lower forms of animal life into complete humans, "five-men," as they called themselves, proudly holding up five misshapen fingers rather than hoof or claw. But because it was an unprecedented social experiment (with some interesting biological dimensions), under controlled conditions established by the military occupiers, Japanese were made into unwilling objects, to be sculpted like clay and hopefully to become one day full-fledged democratic subjects. The occupation seemed most determined to preserve Benedict's image of Japanese and in the process reduced the population to the status of second class clients, perpetually waiting for recognition of full equality which never comes, who, in the eyes of many critics, were literally "deformed," "bent," "disfigured," and made alien to themselves. The constitution the Americans wrote for the Japanese guaranteed fundamental rights absent in the previous Meiji Constitution of Imperial Japan, and gave the Japanese the gift of Article 9 that foreswore war, its principal, democratic legacy (now under serious threat of revision). But the Occupation at the same time decided to retain the emperor (Hirohito) rather than trying him as a war criminal, effectively setting the stage for the undoing of democratization (not to mention subjectivity) which ultimately resulted in the establishment—with American help—of a one party rule that has lasted for nearly a half a century and whose longevity record is matched only by the Mexican PRI. This active undermining of democratization—but not capitalism—is mirrored in the contemporary American reliance on the Iraqi Baathist party to administer the country, lacking yet at the time of this writing the reinstatement of Saddam Hussein.

In short, the American Occupation narrative sought to "remake" Japan as a "free" and "democratic society," and thereby to restore an earlier course which, it was believed, had been diverted in the 1930s. Hence, its plot-line, resituating a capitalist organization of production, displaced certain narrative roles such as the labor strike, to satisfy and even accommodate shifts within American policy toward Japan in 1947 and 1948. Whereas the military administration had no need to account for the reasons prompting Japan to go to war, the subsequent modernizing storyline was obliged to construct an explanation that might simultaneously represent the recent historical experience as a manifestation of the laws of continuous evolutionary adaptive upgrading and persuasively clarify the reasons why Japan went against its liberal political endowment. This required showing that Japan had been temporarily stalled from realizing its true democratic calling because of "structural dysfunctions" produced by an immature social system that had failed to buffer stress and strains. (Thus the reason for the Occupation's emphasis on developing a small-scale capitalist class as against monopolists and cartelists, who were, in any case, all eventually returned.) The argument managed to ratify a functionalist conception for the social order that seemed to have more in common with a modern plumbing system and clogged pipes than a human society.

But Japan was reunited with its democratic mission under the tutelage of a military occupation. The values of instrumental rationality, derived from the fantasy image of a market attentive to small producers and businesses, and the progressive modernization of means were reread as "democratic." Much of the impulse for this approach, deliberately intended to uphold Japan as a showcase of modernization, was thus provided by the "experience" of the occupation and its decision to remake Japanese society after 1947. In fact, the Occupation was retroactively seen as a vital historical episode, if not stage, in Japan's modernization process. It was systematized and given additional empirical authority through the appropriation of a model of development and the research and writing of a generation of specialists who quickly retold the nation's history as a triumphalist transformation enabled through the agency of adaptation and value integration. As envisaged by proponents of Japan's modernization, the nation's history showed how society had peacefully and successfully evolved from a feudal order, whose values had survived to mediate the social changes inflicted by history, and whose more degraded remnants would be eventually eliminated by the dissolving agent provided by Levy's "universal solvent" of rationality. (But no such dissolution of unrational institutions and practices ever took place, as evidenced by the eagerness of the American occupation authorities to retain the emperor, a throwback to an archaic, agrarian order, and the panoply of beliefs, values and rituals associated with it.) Later, this particular role enacted by sturdy traditional values, the force of a feudal unconscious surviving and even exceeding history, encouraged Japanese to appeal to an exceptionalist culture to explain to the world their unique economic and technological achievements in the postwar period. In this sense, the occupation became the vanishing mediator of Japan's postwar history. Paradoxically, the very feudal unconscious Marxists had once identified as the cause of Japan's uneven development and its social contradictions leading to fascism and imperialism now became the principal reason for Japan's modernization.

In the hands of ardent modernizers, Japan's stretchable culture provided analogues to the rationality that had once made the West the best. Modernizers looked to the enthronement of reason and its political management in the present, especially, as the surest sign of Japan's successful development and the meaning of its history. This argument filtered into popular literature in the 1960s and 1970s when widely read novels featured as characters the founder of the Tokugawa shogunate—Ieyasu—and other resourceful administrators and entrepreneurs to show how modern, managerial skills had already been developed in Japan's pre-modern history. The importance of this heavy emphasis on the availability of rational leadership enabled the portrayal of Japanese society to appear as conflict free and consensual, and, in time, as superior and an even more efficient representation of liberal democracy. (It is still hard for me to imagine

why anybody took seriously Ezra Vogel's book of the
1970s, *Japan as Number One*.) In the formulations of
Bellah's powerful and seductive *Tokugawa Religion*
(published first in 1957), appropriating the Parsonian
theory of action, the primacy of political and adaptive
values is located in traditional religious practices.
Bellah observed that this evolved penchant for politics
represented the primacy of particularistic rather than
universalistic values as Weber and Parsons understood
them (lodged in the economy), and showed already
their great pliability and elasticity to accommodate
changes in the environment. In the sphere of religio-
cultural values, Bellah believed he had found the form
of pre-modern rationality—what he reassuringly
referred to as the "functional analogue to the
Protestant ethic." In this way, Japan's traditional religions prefigured, before modernity, the identity of
those rationalizing tendencies that would supply the
necessary motivation for inducing Japanese to accept
the challenge of making vital changes in the interest of
collective survival. Where Weber had linked religion
and economy, Bellah underscored the partnership of
religion and politics. With this realignment, Bellah
provided a strong argument for empowering what
were identified as traditional values, which, despite
risking reification, were mobilized because they had
been able to survive over the long historical duration
by making necessary adjustments. Here, he came
closer to Benedict than he would have wanted to
acknowledge. Such values also attested to the braiding
between norms functioning to secure integration and a
society's aptitude for absorbing the shock wave of

modernizing changes without resorting to disruption and violence.

Later, Bellah, anticipating Inkeles and Davis, proposed that the problem of modernity was not in the circumstances of political and economic systems but in an identity found only in "spiritual phenomena" and "varieties of mentalities." The change toward the modern thus demanded a "social psychological revolution." Yoking rationalization to religio-cultural values was intended to provide a persuasive explanation for showing how tradition mediated social change: the force of evolutionary continuity and consensus over the spectacle of conflict and rupture. But it also cleared the way to an instrumentalization of culture itself to which Japanese increasingly resorted in any attempt to justify the apparent surrender of democratic promise in the 1960s. In this discourse, the wider global arena of Japan's economic hegemony was attributed to the superiority of irreducible cultural traditions. At that time there was a rush to emulate Japan and to discover the "secrets" of what people believed to be its staggeringly spectacular success, resulting in the circulation of all kinds of nonsensical nostrums and snake-oil formulas promising to boost sagging national economies. But the path was blocked because the country's culture was indelibly unique, inaccessible to others and could not be reproduced elsewhere. In this scenario, we must call attention to the fact while Japan's modernization was fueled by traditional cultural values, its achievement reflected the primacy of what Parsons proposed as "particularism" over "universalism," the latter of which both Weber and Bellah identified with the West.

This was a proper explanatory conclusion of Japan's successful modernization and a reflection of its willingness to accept the secondary status of being a client to the American imperium.

If Bellah advanced a persuasive theory of rational action, E.O. Reischauer furnished a supplementary but crucial conceptualization of political leadership. Reischauer, a former professor at Harvard and ambassador to Japan during the Kennedy administration, relied on Rostow's manifesto to show how Japan had masterfully managed to avoid the excesses of conflict and political totalitarianism in the passage to a modern order. In a certain sense he tried to whiten out the very history Barrington Moore had inscribed as the cause of Japan's drift to fascism in the 1930s. But Reischauer's views also brought into consideration the formulations of sociologists like Eisenstadt and Shils, not to forget the anthropologist Clifford Geertz, whose research program (at the University of Chicago) on new nations had already identified the singular importance of the role played by Westernized, read as rational, intellectuals and political leaders in the modernizing process. Hence, Reischauer, by fastening on to the primacy of politics and elite leadership, departed somewhat from Rostow's model, inasmuch as he (Rostow) had accentuated the priority of economic growth leading to political democracy. With this step, Reischauer was persuaded to reassert the central importance of both the state and its bureaucratic management of the economy (capitalism) as the sign of mature, rational political democracy. For societies that had lagged in the quest for modernization (Nazi

Germany, Fascist Italy, the Soviet Union, and militaristic Japan), the disruption revealed "political polarization" which, accordingly, originated in a commitment to rapid (revolutionary) development rather than evolutionary growth characterizing the "democratic states of Western Europe, North America, Australia, and New Zealand." Already committed to the mediating efficacy of traditional values, principally evolved from political values that guaranteed the realization of group consensus, Reischauer claimed that even late developers like Japan, despite the momentary aberration of war with the United States, had avoided revolutionary upheaval because of the adaptive powers of the received endowment. In this view, Japan was not other to the U.S., as Bellah had already verified, and, instead, shared an identity with it. "From the standpoint of world history," Reischauer once told a Japanese audience,

> the most important thing has been the history of Japan in the last 90 years....The reason for this is because it accelerated the modernizing process and used...the pattern of the West. But because it realized great success that it is unique with [sic]. There are a number of trouble problems, such as militarism, but if seen from a broader perspective, Japan is a success. The case of Japan should become a textbook case for the developing nations.

But, as Reischauer already knew, the "textbook" example offered by Japan was inaccessible to Third World imitation since it was locked in a tradition made only by an exceptionalist culture.

V: MODERNIZATION REDUX: WANTING EMPIRE

If the Vietnam War ultimately made a mockery of the social scientific claims for modernization and development, the collapse of the Berlin Wall signaling the end of the Cold War reinforced its final, apparent inutility. It also seemed to induce social science to turn away from the delirium of engineering large scale social change based on a putative theory of rational action and abandon culture and tradition altogether for the equally fanciful desire for a more individualized rationality of choice governing the routines of everyday life everywhere and at any time. (This is not to say that rational choice is free from the illusion of wanting to organize the globe.) In a world no longer polarized as before, thrust into a competition devoted to winning over the unaligned, there was no longer any necessity for modernization and development. The conjuncture of the 1960s, condensed in the world wide movements of '68 starting in Paris incited by the Vietnam War, had called for self-determination in the Third World, and thus delivered the first blow to the imperial claims of modernization, even though it continued to rattle into the decades of the '70s and '80s. But this is not to forget that the binary principle was rescued from discredit and actually resuscitated with the formation of a new and even more dangerous polarity between the United States and the world, especially that portion that has remained outside of the client states constituting the so-called coalition of the willing, the United Kingdom, Australia, Japan, South Korea, Italy.

The sputtering of modernization theory echoed merely the efforts of social science to tighten up the model, fine tune it to meet the exigencies heaved up by the conjuncture, without completely overhauling or abandoning it. But in the world of the late 1960s and 1970s, all of the certain conceits that once energized modernization theory and its developmental impulse were put into question—consensual social systems, democracy and national self determination, free markets, liberal pluralism and its tolerance for difference. In the wake of the Vietnam War and world wide social movements demanding the liberation of the Third World from new forms of imperialism (World Bank, IMF, WTO, etc.) new agendas appeared, devoted to pursuing the claims of gender, sexuality, different subject positions, unmasking the relationship of power/knowledge, and insisting on a reconsideration of the record of colonialism in light of recognized post-colonial misery and immiseration, all fortified by new interpretative strategies and a revitalization of Marxism in the former colonies. (This is not to trivialize the "cultural turn" in Marxism represented by Fredric Jameson, Terry Eagleton, and others, but this wish, after all, was simply a deepening of what was then being called "Western Marxism" and its own obsession to reaffirm a fictional unity and make a last ditch stand in defense of the West at the precise moment when it was being discounted in the Third World for its ethnocentrism.)

The Renewed Assault on the West

For our purposes the major casualty of this conjunc-
tural implosion of older social, political, and cultural
pieties was the withdrawal of the confidence that had
once empowered categorical unities like the West and
the collapse of the authority invested in them. This
withdrawal led to the re-articulation of an assault on
the West and its universalistic claims which, in many
ways, recalled the response of all those societies who
first entered into the world of capitalism at an earlier
time. While the Japanese led this attack with their call
to overcome modernity before World War II, there
was also the example of colonial protest movements
based on preserving what was considered irreducible
native sensibilities before the leveling impulse of capitalist abstraction to destroy difference. In the period
after 1945, the idea of the West, it is well to remember, was a powerful enabling category for both the
Cold War and the formulation of the modernization
program. It was inseparable from the creation of area
studies and constituted the positive pole to its negative
shadow called the "non-West," whose vast, darkened
regions had become the vocation of a social scientifi-
cally driven curriculum and research practicum in
American colleges and universities. Owing to this
relationship between area studies and modernization
theory and practice, as suggested above, the status of
imperialism and colonialism rarely surfaced for serious
consideration and when it did pop up it invariably
appeared as an agent of the modernizing process *avant*

la lettre. This vacated terrain was ultimately filled by facilitating the formation of colonial and post-colonial discourse, a product of the post-Vietnam period inaugurated with the publication of Edward Said's timely book, *Orientalism*, in 1978. Colonial and post-colonial discourse managed to demolish the presumed distinction between West and non-West (even though Said tenaciously clung to it) and the privileged geopolitical identification between modernity and a specific location empowered to assist the rest of the world to catch up.

Despite the impact of post-colonial discourse on the settled practice of area studies and its informing purpose, the idea of a unified "West" has still not disappeared, as it continues to haunt a particular form of cultural Marxism (the signature of the *New Left Review* and its editorial "fight club") and animate the extreme right to newer, loftier heights of phantasmagoric Spenglerian struggle between civilizations where the air has decidedly thinned out. Notably represented by the near hysterical warnings of Theodore von Laue and Huntington, what these and other appeals to a fetishized "West" accomplish with the help of a completed post-colonial discourse, according to Neil Lazarus, is the identification of modernity with Westernization (as did the Japanese in the famous symposium of 1942, titled "Overcoming the Modern") rather than merely capitalism. Huntington, as we saw, was a committed proponent of modernization, which he has differentiated from "Westernization" that he sees now under seige by the very modernizing process he once advocated. In many ways, his attraction to a culturally unified and spatially distinct domain has recuperated the older division of West and non-West and given area studies a momentary stay of execution.

If area studies and modernization theory remain faithful to cultural holism and the identification of core values, effacing along the way both capitalism and imperialism, post-colonial discourse and its unspent desire to account for the complex relationship between colonizer and colonized, metropole and colony, chronology and epistemology, and the past and the present of the postcolony has inadvertently foregrounded the "adverse consequences" caused by the very bracketing of the role played by the agency of capitalism in structuring the imperialist and colonial project. In fact, post-colonial studies since Said's intervention has invariably substituted modernity for capitalism and summoned the category of "the West" to stand in for imperialism. But this slight departure from the practice of area studies seemed to have constituted a quantum leap that opened up an immense, uncultivated terrain that eventually would offer both the availability of a perspective from which to launch a penetrating critique of the destructive consequences of imperialism and colonialism and a window of opportunity for settling scores. In spite of the determination of post-coloniality to uncover the depredations of imperialist and colonial power—what Frantz Fanon once described as the "sacking of cultures of reference," Said made no effort to remove the categorization of the West from his meditations on the "Orient," even though he had explicitly warned

against the ideological freight it took on board. (Only
the Japanese Takeuchi Yoshimi in the immediate postwar period saw how the concept of the "East" was an
effect of the "West" and, according to Naoki Sakai,
co-figured with it.) Yet, it is nevertheless true that
post-colonial studies has not simply demonstrated
admirable sensitivity to the consequences of imperial
colonialism long silenced by area studies and modernization theory but also made available a forum for the
hitherto voiceless to speak in their own voice from the
excluded margin, where domination and power held
them since the beginning of capitalist modernity. In
this regard post-colonial studies has validated its claim
to become the true successor of area studies. Even so,
the desire to settle accounts and redress the imbalance
has been dogged and even compromised by the failure
to divest its own reliance on a unified West, even as it
announces a program to "provincialize Europe" and
"unthink Eurocentrism." The consequences of dema-
terializing capitalist agency for the neutrality of
"modernity" invites both the return of the "West" as a
structuring unity and a reconsideration of its colonial
history now as lasting heritage for the postcolony. By
retreating to the geopolitical space of Euro-America
and the "West," instead of resorting to temporally
fluid categories like capitalism as a globally, structuring agent, as Lazarus has pointed out, post-colonial
discourse risks recuperating the very location of
achievement that has driven writers like Huntington
and von Laue to see in the "West" and "Westernization" the source of universal value. With the removal
of the Soviet Union from the contest for global

supremacy, the United States became the principal custodian of Western Civilization against the negativity of a non-West it once sought to win over. Under this new historical dispensation, modernization theory made a comeback by reuniting with an imperialism and colonialism it had previously misrecognized as development. At this point the ideology of modernization became indistinguishable from the epistemology of empire.

The logic of modernization, and its heavy commitment to an evolutionary narrative, would uphold the importance of maintaining a continuity from colonial status to post-colonial nation. When analysts turned their sights on the nation they would underscore the political and economic achievements of the colonizing state and apprehend this moment retrospectively as the heritage for the future—the post-colonial present. Moreover, it was this transubstantiation of the regrettable and adverse legacy of the colonial experience into a prescient modernizing heritage that would supply the arguments for a subsequent counterattack seeking to now compensate for the "excesses" of post-colonial critique. The genealogy of this historiography that today asks for greater respect for the colonial achievement actually predates the collapse of the Soviet Union originating first in social scientific modernization theory, and even prefigured recent attempts to rescue colonialism's accomplishments for the present and its future.

Colonialism as Modernization

As early as the pivotal decade of the 1960s, social scientists like S.N. Eisenstadt were already assimilating the
experience of colonialism to the modernizing process.
The argumentation was reworked as late as the mid-
1980s by political scientists like David Apter.
Eisenstadt (in 1966) saw the force of colonialism as an
initial agent in the transformation of colonial societies,
what he referred to as the "process of modernization in
so-called new states…." Colonially driven modernization, he acknowledged, was the most "extreme example" because it was induced by "external forces." The
locus of such change was limited to the cities or new,
modern centers which had been directly produced by
the colonial power, narrow in scope, inasmuch as they
were restricted to administrative and technical rather
than cultural and social domains. Moreover, these
urban sites were disposed to further differentiating the
center (the place of modernization) from the periphery—the local level of village community and custom,
whose received everyday life was deliberately left
intact. For Eisenstadt, this splitting constituted a
contradiction between the desire to install a modern
administrative system and new economic and political
infrastructure at the same time that the countryside
would continue to remain exempted from modernizing
changes. The contradiction was reflected in what
Eisenstadt called "unbalanced change" but more properly could be renamed as uneven development. (It is
striking how modernization theorists always assumed

the perfection of even development in the modular and industrialized West when even the most untrained ethnographic eye would immediately recognize the existence of vast patches of uneven terrain in the heart of the most advanced cities and know instinctively that the spectacle illustrated one of the basic laws of capitalism.) While he overlooked the manifestation of unevenness by making it appear as a result of colonialism, he saw its existence as a framework for the development of "indigenous forces of modernization," such as new political elites and the growth of a modern entrepreneurial sector within the traditional colonial setting. Political elites were especially important for Eisenstadt, as they were for the new nations group, principally because of their broader participation in national politics and their role in decolonization and independence. Even more, their importance to the new nation lay in their familiarity with "Westernized values" and experience in "modern institutions" which ultimately enabled them to recognize that the acquisition of such an outlook could not be realized in a colonial context. Although Eisenstadt perceived the natural limits of indigenous groups to develop "new, autonomous orientations to modern frameworks and goals," these "Westernized" intellectuals, what the French have called évolvés, the evolved ones, acting exactly as the neutral, free floating intellectuals envisaged by Karl Mannheim to staff state planning agencies as "scientific managers," would remain vitally important to the modernizing process during and after decolonization. Significantly, new forms of anti-colonial nationalist movements strove to implant newer symbols of solidarity that promised to sidestep the constraints of the colonial context at the same time they failed to overcome the problems caused by unevenness—owing to the "weakness" of economic and professional organization. The import of this observation is the identification of colonial agency in initiating a modernizing process as able to reinforce the division between a growing modern sector and a static traditional one—center and periphery—as envisaged by Shils and expanded upon by Wallerstein in the cause of a different kind of historical sociology. Its legacy for the future would be conveyed by the social group committed to "Western" values and ideologies, not to forget its utopian ambition.

Eisenstadt's account was strongly committed to seeing the necessity of a developmental continuity that ipso facto and unavoidably connects the colonial past to a decolonized present and future. This particular argument was put forth more enthusiastically twenty years later by political scientists like David Apter and became a staple of subsequent approaches to the "developmentalist state." Apter's book *Rethinking Development* (1987) offered a conception of "neo-modernization" and its timing couldn't have been worse or better, depending upon one's perspective, since the case for modernization and development ceased to make sense after 1989 as it moved to a new register to join forces with globalization, then with imperialism and the quest for a new American imperium. Apter transferred the discussion from what he named as "modernization I," a well-meaning liberal discourse fettered to the "realization of developmental growth" through mechanisms of cultural, social, and behavioral adaptation of tradition, functionally emphasizing "their concrete variability" to a new level called "modernization II" that might provide a platform from which to distinguish conflict and violence and the operation of externally imported coercion, capitalist and imperialist, in the preoccupation with institutional legitimacy. But it is not at all clear why Apter insists on calling this new phase modernization II since in doing so he has insured its continuity with a prior discourse or stage of development even as he seems to be trying to sneak in fugitive Marxian insights. Moreover, the recognition of conflict was already inherent in "modernization I," and even writers like Shils and Eisenstadt were willing to acknowledge the instance of protest and conflict in the initial modernizing stages. With Apter the impulse to recuperate developmentalism is still retained regardless of his attempt to add violence and resistance to the mix.

For our purposes, in any event, Apter has simply reaffirmed an older analytic, which he once fully embraced, by restoring its exemplars, so to speak, and pouring into them enriched additives in the attempt to rescue modernization from its theory lite status. Whatever else we may think of this practice, he asserted, "colonialism demonstrated the role of commerce and bureaucracy in modernization," a sentiment resembling older plaints which proudly announced that Mussolini drained the marshes around Rome and made the trains run on time and Hitler built the *autobahn*. As Aimé Césaire reminded us years ago, European colonialism also gave us genocide. In this re-formulation, "political modernization" meant the formation of a "Westernized" political class—secular and prepared to participate in national political life and made available "Western-ized" institutions of governmentality permitting accessibility and representation. For Apter colonialism constituted an historical stage of "transition"—a "universal pattern" in modernization leading to national independence, driven by a dialectic of modernity and traditionalism. But in the end it is the agency of colonialism that initiates the ensuing dialectic, to comprise the "primary instruments of modernization." Here are its narrative themes: "pioneering, bureaucratic, representative and responsible governmental stages." Hence, "colonialism is an interesting historical phase. It illustrates a particular pattern of transition—a pattern in which modernization has been universalized and in which some important roles of modernity have been acquired." (Once more the appeal to "transition" as an explanatory category masquerading for unevenness manages only to appear as a ghostly reminder of its analytic emptiness.) In Apter's scenario, modernization merges politically and economically with the achievement of decolonization, now acting in concert to stage colonialism as a necessary historical condition of modernity and making it appear inseparable from the steps by which the colony evolves into nationhood.

This yearning to fasten colonization to modernization obviously works to cement the role of continuity between past and present that supplies both the framework for developmentalist claims (role of the state, bureaucracy, "westernized" entrepreneurs all deriving from the colonial episode) and a fetishization of the origin of the later nation state which, it is argued today, would not have been possible without this legacy. But for this kind of developmental argument to work, whether concentrating on the Japanese or British empires, still necessitated casting the colonial period into the pre-given role of playing the traditional past of the colony that progressively led to the modern present. This argument was raised early by analysts of East Asian societies who saw in Japan's colonial adventures the same signs of prescient rationality observed in the nation's modernizing history. Colonialism thus became an explanation for the later economic (not necessarily political) growth in former colonies like South Korea and Taiwan. Their putative economic miracles were said to reflect Japanese investments and the development of an industrial infrastructure initiated by the empire, which would give the new economies of Taiwan and South Korea a jump start after decolonization. But this contention has been more infamously advanced today by an historiography that wishes to make the case for Great Britain's historical empire as a living heritage for its former colonies and as the mirrored image for the new American imperium to emulate. In its worst form the account projects a retrospective illusion of an imperial past that it seeks to map onto an imagined future. In this new enthusiasm for imperial design, it is important to recognize that any appeal to the Japanese or French models (a former enemy and a supplier of revolutionary strategies in the Third World) might prove to be embarrassing.

Dreaming of Empire Days

Throughout this study the figure of empire, however shadowy, has never been far from the desire of modernization. It has always lurked in the background, as if it was an unconscious veiled by the good intentions of its dreamers and executors. From the accounts that first aimed at explaining America's post-9/11 declaration of war against terrorism the specter of this modernizing impulse has never been very far from policy statements and assessments of policy. The reason this bonding today has been given force and a renewed lease on life in the resurrection of a phantasmagoric British Empire as a foundational historical experience and America's true imperial legacy undoubtedly arises from the tenacious persistence of the Cold War and the strategy to export modernization and development to win over the unaligned. This goal, as we have seen, was the pursuit of political stabilization among the new, unaligned nations in order to realize an hegemony capable of guaranteeing the maintenance of America's privileged economic status. In other words, modernization, today renamed as "regime change," was inseparable from the Cold War. The subsequent collapse of the Soviet Union (mythologized as Ronald Reagan's triumph) did not necessarily entail formulating new policy strategies but only re-adapting older ones to new global circumstances. In re-writing the script communism was replaced by terrorism, paradoxically making a method into an ideology, and effectively retaining the received

binary between "good" and "evil." The signs of this
re-articulation were already apparent in the latter days
of the Cold War, during Reagan's presidency, when
policy turned to accelerating struggle by resorting to
war by proxy. These proxy wars invariably obliged the
United States to rely on enlisting terroristic groups,
whose talents for terror were sanitized to make them
look like freedom fighters, as in Afghanistan, and to
sponsor right wing regimes in Africa and Latin
America by renaming them as democracies. But the
aim of a strategy to employ proxies was no different
from the imperial aspirations built into earlier theorizations of modernization and fashioning of programs
which, as we have seen, were always willing to rally in
defense of imperialism and colonialism as "objective"
stages or even "transitions" in the march of progress.
With the Iraq War and the military occupation of the
country, the United States has moved from orchestrating proxy wars to carrying out full scale territorial
seizure (however momentary) to provide authority to
the relationship between empire and modernization
that the Cold War successfully disguised by overstat-
ing the Soviet Union's ideological mission of world
conquest and the threat of its military capability to
achieve it. The American intervention in Iraq, especially, re-introduced the silhouette of empire into the
popular and journalistic imagination, as well as in the
more scholarly discussions, and encouraged the desire
of supplying it with an historical model of proper
moral purpose rather than simple naked self-interest.
It is in this particular context that the overheated
resuscitation of the old British Empire days has been

aroused from its slumber in historical mothballs to demonstrate its succession in the contemporary American imperium but also its immediate necessity since the United States has now inherited the duty to defend the values of the Western (white man's) civilization against persisting axes of evil, just as the British had once envisioned this task as its aptitude for empire. Here are the real lessons of history. But celebration of the British Empire today is sparked as much from an insurmountable nostalgia for the vanished dominations of empire days as it reflects the conviction that empire is always the vehicle of modernization.

Safely closeted in history's dust bin, the British Empire has now become the commodity for a new industry devoted to glamorizing imperial heritage and offers the United States a harmless and more benign model for imitation and legitimacy. In fact, the argument easily makes the United States the successor of the old British Empire and the inheritor of its modernizing mission. In the current rush to reclaim the benefits of the imperial form for the U.S. the British template has become the favored candidate for two reasons: (1) the U.S. is seen to have filled the vacuum left by the dissolution of the British Empire over a half a century ago and has willingly accepted the "responsibility" for its dispersal; and (2) the succession offers a presumed continuity between Great Britain's non-revolutionary political tradition and its constitutional "gift" to its former colonies and the American preoccupation, since the time of the occupation of Japan, with spreading democracy (with market capitalism). The presentation of America's new imperium by its authors suggests both "denial" and the promotion of a developmental desire driven only by a "benevolent" ambition to spread modernization in the form of democratizing the globe and its accompanying marketization. The imperium, in this sense, is inseparable from the American nation itself, its values and ethos, the whole historical tradition of expansionism mediated by the most pious moralism (think of the Monroe Doctrine) that laid hold of a continent before looking outward, as well as its reincarnation in modernizing and developmental strategies, whose fulfillment, it was believed, can only make a better world.

But we must ask why imperialism—new, old, or indifferent—has now climbed aboard the contemporary agenda when only a few years ago it was safely restricted to historical exegeses, dull monographs or subjected to a penetrating critique of its predatory practices, gratuitous violence and senseless dehumanization. Why indeed are we currently drawn into a reconsideration of imperialism as if it were an old forgotten friend? Arundhati Roy, writing in *The Nation*, has recently wondered why people are now "openly talking about the good side of imperialism and the need for a strong empire to police an unruly world." But she rightly reminds us that "debating imperialism is a bit like debating the pros and cons of rape" and that we are made to believe it is something that we have long missed and now yearn to recover. But as we shall see, even historical scholarship has been enlisted into the cause of rescuing empire from its post-colonial battering in order to speak about the good side of imperialism. Under the guise of historical scholarship there has been a steady revival of imperialism and learned reappraisals of the British Empire in an environment consecrated to upholding it as the candidate of choice for figuring and justifying the new American imperium. The BBC's fatal talent for aestheticizing the national past, after its successful and popular walk down World War I's memory lane, has recently been turned to lovingly recounting the splendor and glory of the Empire. This new sentimental journey aims to recapture imperial aura for a generation that no longer has any real recollection of it. In this respect, the output of recent historiography shares in this attempt to put a better face on the Empire by resuscitating its lost glitter. The pursuit takes different shapes but it invariably leads to extolling the accomplishments of empire. Linda Colley, concentrating in her recent book, *Captives*, on the relationship between Great Britain's smallness (population, land space, etc) and the largeness of its eventual empire, proposes that the empire was as much captive as captor. While she willingly acknowledges all of the known abuses inflicted by the British on colonized peoples she also wants to suggest that the detrimental aspect of colonialism is still not a known quantity as once believed and that further research is necessary to understand how the lives of the "small people" were affected and altered. The point to her long meditation on captivity narratives is to remind us that the imperial invaders were victims of their conquest in ways that have rarely been the subject of serious historical inquiry. The theme of her study is actually imperial co-dependency, whereby the British were seen to be as dependent upon both native elites and subject peoples to run and maintain their empire as they were on the good will of their "small people," whose stories reveal what they sacrificed. British lives were irretrievably changed and even destroyed by their involvement in the imperial project. But what seemingly is displaced in this well-intended plea for more research that will tell a fuller story is the fact of imperial intervention itself which is not made any more acceptable by easy avowals that recognize that the British were captives of their empire, codependent on their colonial subjects, who, in turn, become implicated in their own subjugation. In this regard, the fuller story has already been achieved in acknowledging the forcible intervention of British imperial ambitions. Nor is this intervention made more acceptable by asserting that the enterprise was not simply the work of a few gentlemanly capitalists but enlisted the support of the "small people" without whose assent it would not have been possible. This impulse paradoxically portrays the general population as both willing and complicit agents and self-sacrificing victims. (Apparently, smallness wins no immunities from historical judgment!) In any event, these, and more, are the real, unstated lessons empire supposedly teaches and which, as we've seen in the modernization process, constitute a "heritage" for the future post-colony. But for Colley, the lessons to be learned by the United States as it dons the garb of its new imperial fashion in the twenty-first century are ones of balance and awareness of what it means to avoid the status of becoming a captive of the "conquered," as both Great Britain in Afghanistan in 1842 and the United States in Iran in 1979-81 experienced as parallel imperial traumas. Britain's immense empire resulted from the smallness of the home country and its status as a maritime nation and suggests that the largeness of the United States, which is land based, has no need for further territorial seizure and acquisition. If, as she claims, the model Britain offers is one that acknowledges the relationship between size, "levels of ambition and power," keeping its empire within bounds and which America now threatens to exceed, the real point of this defense of empire that pleads for more historical knowledge at the same time she wishes to implicate the "small people" and their stories would have served history better had she concentrated on precisely the conditions that pressed them into complicity in the first place.

With David Cannadine's *Ornamentalism: How The British Saw Their Empire* there is a more explicit desire to seize the enunciative voice, as it were, and take back the power of representation colonial discourse and post-colonial theory have seemingly captured in recent years. Cannadine wants to turn the table and redress what he plainly perceives is the imbalance created when the subaltern was actually allowed to break her/his silence and speak. His project wishes to illustrate how the British saw their empire, while his pursuant goal is to contest the Saidian conviction that such perceptions were driven by racism and forms of "othering." Hence, "Empire was not exclusively...about what the British decided and did: it was about assorted and multifarious experiences of many peoples in many parts of the world whom the British encountered, domesticated, damaged and grudgingly set free." (Perhaps this constitutes simply another way of calling attention to imperial co-dependency.) New post-imperial historiography of India, especially, has envisaged Britain's intervention as a disaster. To offset this unflattering view, Cannadine offers an account that takes into consideration the "vast interconnected world" that integrated the metropole and its colonies, which in turn, permits the perspective of actually considering the nature of the imperial experience and what the empire looked like. In other words he advances a social history of the empire, which means a conception of empire founded on the "vernacular image of domestic, ranked social hierarchy." As a result, the empire was determined to assimilate the colonies to the metropolitan vision of status quo, what Cannadine calls "the replication of sameness and similarities." For this reason he proposes that the empire was less involved in the "creation of othering" as imagined by Said and his followers than it was with the "construction of affinities." The lingering traces of the social hierarchy lived by colonizer and colonized are still etched in the decolonized states of the empire. In South Asia and Malaysia the former ruling hierarchs have retained both their fortunes and their social status, presumably entitlements from the colonial past.

Even elsewhere Cannadine has observed the persisting vestiges of a still intact social hierarchy—the Queen still remains the head of the state in former

dominions (mostly white settler colonies) and there
seems to continue a sharing of hierarchical attitudes
between the crown and its former peers in the
colonies. Cautiously, Cannadine concludes that even
though the British Empire is now gone, it has not
entirely "vanished from the mind…and elsewhere, too,
its hierarchical sentiments, and some of its structures
endure." His reasoning is rooted in the assumption
that while empire's social order was rejected, along
with the dissolution of its enabling structures, there
still lingers the nostalgia for the idea of social order
itself that reflected its "vast, interconnected world"
and expresses the personal conviction that its ideality
continues to exist in the mind's memory. It should be
pointed out that Cannadine's interpretation hinges on
the belief that the British related to, say, the Indian
ruling classes because of their own hierarchical world-
view, that they could match status with status or, at
least, see similarities between the two social orders,
surely a promising candidate for the overlooked category of vulgar Weberianism. In this account race,
then, is demoted for status (and possibly class?) but it
fails to show that this imperial tactic of eliciting coop-
eration of local elites had more to do with exercising
control and expropriation than recognizing social
equals. It was a tactic that had early recognized the
numerical inferiority of the invading force and quickly
turned to soliciting support from local rulers who, for
a variety of reasons, were all too happy to cooperate
against their masses in the subsequent expropriation of
resources. Moreover, it also failed to lessen any
expression of racial superiority. Perhaps he would

have benefited from Colley's book coming out before his. Nevertheless, the powerful traces of empire and the priority it accorded to status—that is social order itself—linger on like a bad tune or house odor. Cannadine concludes by saying that while the dominions had followed the American model—democratic and anti-hierarchical—many of the former colonies favored the "milder Indian variant of independence and social revolution," retaining, nonetheless, some of the emblems of similarity that once guaranteed the identity of metropole with colony. What seems to have been communicated is how a colonial heritage devoted to social order still persists throughout much of the formerly colonized world of the empire and that a continuity between this past and the present is its lasting achievement.

If Cannadine and Colley timidly signify luke-warm attempts to restore the empire to good historio-graphical standing, still a warm-up to the main event, the historian Niall Ferguson has made this crusade into an ideological battle cry in a tireless effort to encourage the United States to continue pursuing its imperial interest as long as it follows the precedents established by Britain's Empire of the last century. In Ferguson's sleight of hand, the older modernization narrative is conjured up to appear as the historical calling of empire whose contemporary embodiment in the American imperium must continue to fulfill its mission as a modernizing agent. But the violence leaking out from the facade of Ferguson's historical scholarship stretches the capacity for credulity and might even prompt some to wonder about the kind of socialization that has molded this outlook. The really important question raised by this point of view relates less to personal and careerist motivations than to the reasons why institutions like *The New York Times* and elite private universities in the United States have so enthusiastically and continuously endorsed such a dangerous mindset and what their stakes are in continually rewarding it.

Ferguson's successful TV series and resulting book called *Empire* has aimed to show how empire had become a valued heritage, especially as it was accomplished on the cheap. His numerous articles in the media and regular appearance in *The New York Times* have repetitively hammered on this theme and, along the way, affirmed the steady rightward rush of the newspaper and a lowering, if not cheapening, of its already compromised journalistic standards. Bolder and more prone to provocation than Cannadine, and certainly more excitable (it's almost possible to imagine skulking in the background the sophomoric socialization of Oxford speaking unions), he has asserted relentlessly that "without the spread of British rule around the world, it is hard to believe that the structures of liberal capitalism would have been successfully embedded in so many different economies around the world." It is important to recognize prowling in this sweeping effusion yet another sophomoric reflex in his promotion of a "logic" of counterfactuality—the desire for the "but for" that seems to have provided the sole basis for both his proposition that the British Empire was a good thing and the imperative that today it must serve as the inspiration for the United

States. It should be pointed out that counterfactual thinking, apart from its use by a generation of older positivist prone philosophers of science, is principally a tactic deployed in debating to set or change the terms of discussion in one's favor. In fact, it is what drives a debate. We must identify in this unscheduled descent into fantasy an up-to-date version of an earlier penchant of the British ruling class, recorded brilliantly by P.G. Wodehouse, to enthusiastically embrace spiritualism, theosophy, and diverse forms of crack pot mysticism bordering on the hallucinatory.

It is thus Ferguson's concluding remarks, never actually demonstrated in the body of the textual narrative, that without the experience of the British Empire, it is unimaginable that there would have been the spread and establishment of constitutional and deliberative institutions of political democracy—which, again, the United States is now committed to spreading around the globe. "India," he exhorts, "the world's largest democracy, owes more than it is fashionable to acknowledge to British rule." Shadowing Cannadine but unconstrained by his mature sense, he openly charges that its schools, universities, press, and parliamentary system all derive from the British model, as if the older imperial impulse to fix sameness still persisted as an unyielding spectral presence that punctually reappears to remind the present of a glorious past. English, he announces proudly, was taught by the British and is the second language today to nearly a half a billion people. But he is willing to acknowledge that Britain's imperial record was not always "unblemished" and that it had failed to satisfy its own goals of "individual liberty." But tarnished and unfulfilled ambitions notwithstanding, Britain introduced "free trade," "free capital movements," "private investment," and "free labor after it abolished slavery." Again, the counterfactual slide: "There would not have been so much free trade between the 1840s and 1930s had it not been for the British Empire." A sooner, rather than later, relinquishing of colonies would have resulted in disastrous protectionism that would not have been beneficial to the world economy. Because British imperialism came late, it was forced to colonize undeveloped lands in North America, rather than seize populated regions up for easy plunder. (Was India under-populated?) In this regard, Ferguson identifies empire as an agency of development as if this were its principal calling. Development was, moreover, internally expanded because of law and administration—and governance. But the clinching explanation is provided by modernization theory when he cites S.M. Lipset's assertion that former British colonies had a "better chance of achieving enduring democracy after independence" than did any other colonies. All this merely inspires the declaration that imperial forms constitute the model of international governance and thus act as the agent of globalization (one shudders to think what would have happened, say, if the Ottoman Empire had been used for such purposes or even the Hapsburgs but such thinking is mere counterfactual indulgence.) In this view the imperial form offers the best hedge against the political fragmentation of smaller countries that disrupt and impede global growth, an extraordinarily breathtaking blending of Kautsky's "superimperialism" and Hardt and Negri's empire of the multitude. Although the Anglo-phonic economic and political liberalism is the culture of choice of much, if not all of the world, it faces "a serious threat from Islamic fundamentalism." Without the policing of a "formal empire," Ferguson asks rhetorically, "how far can the dissemination of Western 'civilization'—meaning the Protestant, Deist-Catholic-Jewish mix that emanates from modern America— ...safely be entrusted to Messrs. McDonald and Disney?"

It hardly needs saying that this "mix" that now constitutes imperial America is principally white. In his most recent pronouncements, channeled again through *The New York Times*, he has resorted to trying to show the relevance of learning a lesson from the superior example of Britain's historical experience in Iraq (to what? getting out?) to contemporary comparisons with the Vietnam War, which ended in failure and defeat.

All of this brings us back to where we began, as Ferguson summons Robert Cooper's call to "reorder the world" and to "envision a 'defensive' imperialism." "The most logical way to deal with chaos and the one most employed in the past is colonization." Defensive or pre-emptive, it is still imperialism searching for new forms of colonization and military occupation. But Cooper's challenge to envisage a new kind of imperialism dedicated to order and organization, "an imperialism of neighbors" inviting intervention, is not only an exhausted echo of the modernization paradigm now retrofitted to meet the exigencies of "globalization" in a world where only American interests dominate. Even more strangely, it unfortunately hearkens back to the remote past to remind us—Americans—of the Monroe Doctrine. Where Ferguson departs from the "Oxford-educated" imperial unconscious he proudly shares with Cooper and his kind is in his unbound enthusiasm for assigning this role to the United States.

VI: CONCLUSION: HISTORY LESSON

Only the United States is in the position to succeed and replicate the old British Empire and impose its values (really Britain's values) on the underdeveloped non-West—a vocation which, Ferguson surprisingly forgets, had already been promoted by modernization theory and its programs since the end of World War II. Undoubtedly driven by a nostalgia for the lost world of empire, Ferguson rescues its past by making it into an analogy whose timeless lessons the United States must now follow. Like all historical analogies (whose logic is as faulty as the null-hypotheses of counterfactual "reasoning") it ignores the messiness of different temporalizations not even a successful Oxford debater could finesse. In the current discussions, there has been too much of a reliance on the lessons of history offered by appeals to spurious analogies and too little concern for historical understanding. But historical analogies function only to supply lessons to policy makers, who seek the sign of historical authority in order to by-pass history and thereby justify their decisions without any understanding of the historical reasons underlying them.

But the United States has no need for a romantic attachment to analogy derived from another place or time. It certainly has no need to become the successor to the British Empire as designated by nostalgic well-wishers who apparently can't live with its memory alone. And there is no necessity to repeat the dubious lessons of another's history as if, like modernization itself, it was simply a textbook one could consult for faultless instruction and guidance. The United States has only to draw upon its own stockpile of experience amassed by the workings of the modernization paradigm and its seemingly unlimited mandate to promote development everywhere and anywhere. Today the goal is called "globalization," even though the term and the process it names are each fast playing out their doubtful conceptual productivity. Hardt and Negri named it Empire when its constituent patterns seem only to point to yet another form of modernization we might call, *pace* Apter, modernization III. The transmutation was completed at the linguistic level: while modernization and its developmental impulse once employed a benevolent, liberal idiom, using the desire for freedom, democracy, and progress everywhere to deliver America's subliminal imperial aspiration, neo-liberalism today simply acknowledges this ambition openly in the language of naked imperialism, even though it still summons the threadbare rhetoric of democratization.

The evolution of what I have called modernization III represents the latest avatar of a Cold War strategy that set off the massive attempt to transform the uncommitted (the great unknown) into regional outlets of an immense American chain store. In the circumstances of a new stage of struggle against an amorphous terrorism that has no prospect of ever being eliminated since it has no address or real political identity other than its negativity, the United States is now positioned to openly embark upon imperial war and military occupation in order to promote modernizing development which, today, cloaks itself in appeals to democracy and freedom. Its only goal still seems to be the realization of political stabilization under the impetus of Neo-Liberal capitalism in those regions of the world that remain unassimilated to its hegemony or unwilling to join it. The absence of the Soviet Union as a contender and the new crusade has made it possible for the United States to solder imperial design to modernization as if they constituted two sides of the same coin when, before, the imperial impulse was disguised in modernizing developmental policies. The recent revelations of systematic and policy driven torture of Iraqi prisoners simply recall the conduct of empires in the past: France's experience during the Algerian War, for example, and the barbarity of French behavior toward Algerian prisoners. All of those attempts to show how colonial regimes functioned as agents of modernization as if it had been the primary intention all along can neither displace the record of violence nor permit forgetting it as a necessary price for the realization of a greater good. Empires invariably mean entitlements to violence, and especially the "abstraction of violence" produced by capitalism and rationality, and no amount of data attesting to its effectivity or its salutary political legacy or exemplary social history will alter that simple fact. This is the lesson apparently lost to history.

In its new imperial clothes, modernization III also recalls another kind of consequence we are beginning to live today. The violence inflicted on colonized peoples is reflected in programs designed to diminish domestic dissent and curtail individual liberties in the interest of bolstering homeland security. There is an interesting symmetry between the anti-communist domestic terror of the early Cold War years and more recent efforts by the executive branch to exert greater surveillance and control over the civilian population. Through the administration of scheduled and punctual terror alerts the state has virtually routinized fear as the central experience in everyday life. In this nightmarish scenario of modernization III we are returned to the historical scene that presents an enactment of the relationship between imperialism and fascism. As a result, we are left with the certain conviction that it is not possible to escape, as Amin said, "the regression into fascism without breaking categorically with the logic of neo-liberal globalization." Modernization theory and its most enthusiastic proponents have always drawn their self-esteem from looking to the vast, unintended consequences of colonialism and its effect on the development of new nations after decolonization. Yet this desire to soften the violence of the modernizing process by enlisting the agency of foreign domination arises, I believe, from a crucial misrecognition that still persuades the United States to pursue an imperial project devoted to transforming societies and changing regimes in the interest of a higher good. This astigmatic vision prompts an identification of development with capitalism. We know, however, that capitalism is not a "system of development" but rather an abstract tendency and an historical reality that produces capital and augments its unlimited expansion. Development, as conveyed by modernization, is simply an ideological concept that enables the evaluation of results according to a priori criteria conforming to any social program. Where the confusion exists is between the reality of capitalist expansion on the one hand, and what gets counted as a desirable result on the other. The latter, named development, has already been prefigured as a goal. In this combination the very institutions that enhance and enable the expansion of capital, notably the state, identify the desired results by attributing them as instances of development. Yet the logic of capitalist expansion, knowing only the limits of capital itself, can never really imply development because it will always generate unevenness and forms of unequal exchange. Capitalism, for example, is never capable or interested in developing full employment or producing equality in income distribution since expansion is always powered by the pursuit of profit for the state and companies that own them as private property. This is as true of the capitalist engineered theories and programs of modernization envisaged by well meaning liberal social scientists in the United States, as it was for the Stalinist campaign to realize "capitalism without capitalism" in the great stride to catch up with the bourgeois West.

What the older theory of modernization always tried to side step was a fear of the unknown driving its desire to make the world over in the image of capitalist society. But the effort to remake the world inevitably resulted in abstracting what in effect was concrete and different. How could it have been otherwise from such a distant perspective? Hence, the current polarization which pits the United States against that portion of the world it has not yet assimilated to its exemplars. When Dick Cheney expresses his fear of the world, as he has done in order to justify the war in Iraq (or George W. Bush barks "you're either with us or against us"), he is acknowledging the identity between a fear of terrorism and terrorism of fear. Modernization during the Cold War managed to supply a strategy based upon the achievement of a rational (modern) society (actually profit) and the capacity to fix judgmental standards that confidently distinguished civilized from non-civilized life. But its effect was to exalt abstraction over the concrete, the impersonal and rational over the immediately personal and arbitrary. In the end, it sought to extinguish this fear of the unknown by deploying the power of the binary to make the unfamiliar familiar. The national allegory figured by Graham Greene decades ago in his novel, *The Quiet American*, reveals the truth of a past that has not passed: "I never knew a man who had better motives for all the trouble he caused." ∎

TORNADO
ALLEY

White Dove Romances

Tornado Alley
Secret Storm
Mirror of Dreams
Picture Perfect
A Fighting Chance

TORNADO ALLEY

YVONNE LEHMAN

BETHANY HOUSE PUBLISHERS
MINNEAPOLIS, MINNESOTA 55438

Tornado Alley
Copyright © 1996
Yvonne Lehman

Published by Bethany House Publishers
A Ministry of Bethany Fellowship, Inc.
11300 Hampshire Avenue South
Minneapolis, Minnesota 55438

Printed in the United States of America.

Library of Congress Cataloging-in-Publication Data

Lehman, Yvonne.
   Tornado alley / Yvonne Lehman.
      p.   cm. — (White dove romances ; 1)
   Summary: Natalie is asked out by the cool new boy at
school just as her church youth group decides to take vows
of sexual abstinence, and in the tumultuous events that
follow Scott proves he is more than just rich and
handsome.

    [1. Christian life—Fiction. 2. Sexual ethics—Fiction.
3. Tornadoes—Fiction. 4. Family life—Fiction.]
I. Title. II. Series: Lehman, Yvonne. White dove
romances ; 1.
PZ7.L5322To   1996
[Fic]—dc20   95–45108
ISBN 1–55661–705–4   CIP
                                           AC

To
my daughter, Lori,
whose vision and evaluation
have been invaluable
in the preparation and completion
of this book

and to
Anne, Carol, and Barb
for their belief in my ability
with the help of God

and to
Peggy, Lurlene, David, Kellie, Howard, Cindy,
Mary Beth, and Kristina.

YVONNE LEHMAN is the award-winning author of ten published novels, including seven inspirational romances, two contemporary novels, and a biblical novel, *In Shady Groves*. She and her husband, Howard, have four grown children and four grandchildren, and they make their home in the mountains of North Carolina.

One

"Shawnee High, goodbye!" Stick Gordon whooped, slamming his metal locker door shut, making a racket loud enough to burst the eardrums. As if that wasn't enough, he whirled around, tucked his fingers in his armpits, pumped his arms, and began clucking like a chicken.

"Stiiiiiick!" shrieked Natalie Ainsworth as one of his sharp elbows caught her on the arm and knocked her off balance, causing her to drop her books.

"Sorry, sorry," he apologized profusely, jumping back with his hands spread and simultaneously stepping on Ruthie Ryan's toes.

"Ouch, you clumsy oaf!" Ruthie complained. Her brown eyes flashed. "Will you get away from here before you break our bones?"

"On my way . . . on my way," he sing-songed, innocently wide-eyed, and tiptoed around the group of juniors, some laughing, some rolling their eyes in dismay.

Ruthie shook her head of red curls, watching the tall, lanky frame bound down the hallway, then zip around a corner, heading for the gym. She sighed. "It's the same ritual every day after school. Why do we put up with him?"

" 'Cause he's so *cute*!" piped up one of the guys.

"Cute?" asked several of the girls in unison, wrinkling their noses.

Stick's face was all huge dark eyes—and ears, the close-cropped hair around them making them stand out prominently. On top, his crew cut resembled a paintbrush with stiff bristles about three inches long.

"He's okay," said Natalie defensively, rubbing the spot that would probably turn into a nasty bruise. Her deep blue eyes shone with compassion as she thought how Stick's exuberance paid off on the basketball court. Having retrieved her books, she shoved them into her locker.

"Well," conceded Ruthie, her best friend, "we're all glad to hear that last bell of the day."

"Yeah, and besides that, it's hump day!" another added.

While lockers banged and feet scuffed along the hallway that was beginning to clear, the group of juniors chattered about the school year that was drawing to a close. Next year—a much-desired goal—they'd all be seniors.

"Oh," Ruthie wailed, making a tragic face, "don't remind me! Finals are coming up!"

The conversation trailed off as Cissy Stiles approached. She never appeared to walk—she glided, Natalie observed. But what was a senior doing *here*— on the junior floor?

With her cool, sky-blue gaze fastened on Natalie, Cissy asked in her most sugary tone, "Could I see you for a sec?"

"Me?" Natalie squeaked, pointing toward her own chest.

Cissy nodded, not disturbing a single hair of her sleek, sculptured pageboy. The color was to die for—like corn silks on a sunny day. She looked terrific. But Cissy Stiles would look good even if she were bald-headed!

Self-consciously, Natalie flicked at her own light brown hair that fell around her shoulders.

"Um . . . it's about the minutes of the meeting," the older girl added while everyone stared.

"Sure," Natalie mumbled uncertainly, wondering what she'd done so wrong that the student council president would seek her out after school. If Natalie had made a mistake when she read the minutes earlier, why hadn't Cissy brought it up? She certainly wasn't shy.

Cissy tilted her head toward a nearby classroom. "Let's step in there."

"Wait for me, Ruthie?" Natalie asked, seeing the puzzled look in her friend's big brown eyes.

Ruthie's unruly red curls bobbed about her face like unwinding springs. "You bet!" the shorter girl agreed. Then she leaned back against a locker, holding her books in front of her as if nothing could pry her away.

Twila Jones and Maggie Bentley hurried off, eager to escape the confining hallway.

Once inside the classroom, Cissy smiled broadly at the teacher who was sitting behind her desk shuffling papers. "Just conducting a little business, Miss Roper."

"Monkey business?" was the quick reply, but an understanding gleam appeared in the teacher's light gray eyes. She stood and gathered several papers in her hand. "It's all yours. I need to see the principal."

Wow! Natalie thought. She could never be that bold with teachers, no matter how nice they were. But Cissy was used to taking charge. She had even modeled for one of the department stores in the mall. Although Natalie herself was five foot six, Cissy was at least three inches taller, and the effect was daunting.

"I didn't want to talk about the minutes at all," Cissy confessed as soon as Miss Roper disappeared through the doorway. "I just didn't want the others to hear what I had to say." Then she got right to the point. "Do you have a date for the prom? The Junior Prom, I mean."

Was Cissy on the prom committee? If so, maybe she wanted Natalie to pour punch or something. "I've been asked," Natalie replied skeptically, not sure what she was getting at.

The smile left Cissy's face. "Oh." She placed one hand on the hip of her stylish dress. "So you have a date?"

"I haven't given my answer," Natalie admitted. "Actually, I was asked by a couple of guys from church. I've grown up with both of them—you know . . . it would be like going with a brother. I guess I'm not sure yet."

"Perfect!"

Cissy's reaction was surprising. *What is this all about?* Natalie wondered.

"Look," Cissy said, leaning over and lowering her

voice, "my cousin is thinking of asking you."

"Who. . . ?" Natalie began, but before she could get the question out of her mouth, Cissy continued excitedly.

"He just moved here this year, but you might know him—Scott Lambert."

Natalie gazed at her, dumbfounded. Who *didn't* know Scott Lambert—the new guy who had rolled in with the hottest sports car in town? He was the talk of the school for a while. After the novelty died down, though, he'd been labeled nice enough, but too mysterious. The only sport he pursued was track, and he didn't seem to hang out with anyone in particular. Still, the girls had all decided that getting a date with Scott Lambert would be like winning the sweepstakes—one chance in a million!

It occurred to Natalie that Cissy might be playing some kind of game. Maybe she was being initiated into a club that required she perpetrate a cruel joke. Why else would she have picked Natalie? She raised an eyebrow. "Why doesn't he ask me himself?"

Cissy drew her lower lip between perfect white teeth and grimaced. "Oh, he'd kill me if he knew I was doing this. But I wanted to prepare you. He's out of town with his dad all this week, and I was afraid someone else would ask you before he got back."

"I'm sure he'd have no trouble at all getting a date on his own," Natalie blurted out, still skeptical. She hadn't thought of herself as Scott's type.

"Oh, sure, girls die for him," Cissy agreed. "But he's very particular. He looks before he leaps . . . if you know what I mean."

Natalie couldn't help laughing. It was funny, picturing the tall, good-looking Scott Lambert in the midst of a giant leap.

Cissy spread her hands. "He just said he *might* ask you," she emphasized. "I wanted you to know so you wouldn't make a date with anyone else."

Natalie was stunned. She had never had a personal conversation with Cissy, one of the most popular girls at Shawnee High. Now, ignoring the wild thumping of her heart, she spoke as calmly as possible. "Thanks for the information."

"Sure thing, kiddo."

Cissy's flippant remark reminded Natalie that the two of them were not on equal footing. At least today Natalie had worn a pair of carpenter pants and a linen top, since there was a council meeting.

When Cissy reached the doorway, she tossed a warning over her shoulder. "Don't you dare tell him I said anything."

Natalie held on to the doorcasing, staring after Cissy as she breezed down the hallway, so beautiful and confident. Surely she wouldn't be mean enough to play a trick like this!

Seeing Natalie emerge from the empty classroom, Ruthie stepped away from her locker and waved her hand in front of her friend's eyes. "Hey, remember me? I waited. Now, don't you think I deserve an explanation? What did Cissy want? And *who* are you not supposed to tell *what?*"

"Who? What?" Natalie turned to Ruthie and saw the glimmer of mischief in her friend's eyes. She had always told Ruthie everything. Anyway, the news was too great to keep to herself.

"Oh," Natalie tossed out nonchalantly as she tucked a stray lock of hair behind her ear, "just Scott Lambert."

"Scott Lambert?" Ruthie shrieked, her brown eyes threatening to pop out of her freckled face. "What about that hunk?"

"Cissy said he might ask me to the prom."

With that, Ruthie came unglued, her questions pouring forth. "Every word," she demanded. "I want to know every word she said—down to the last lisp."

"Cissy doesn't lisp."

"Well, I can dream, can't I?" Ruthie returned impishly. "Surely she has a fault somewhere. Now, tell me!"

Natalie leaned back against a locker and obliged.

"Cool! Totally awesome!" Ruthie exclaimed, growing more enthusiastic by the moment.

"Oh, come on, Ruthie," Natalie scolded as she strode down the hallway toward the exit. "He's just an ordinary guy. He's not a celebrity or anything."

Ruthie's eyes grew dreamy. "But he looks like one. And that cranberry car. Oh, it's so awesome!"

When they reached the exit, Natalie shoved the heavy door open and stepped out into the warm spring sunshine. She grinned at the statue of the great Shawnee Indian chief, Tecumseh, who at last seemed to have found his niche standing guard at the school entrance. She cut her shining eyes around at Ruthie. "What do I need with a totally awesome cranberry sports car?"

They giggled as they strolled along the walkway outside the school.

"Then you'll say yes, of course!" Ruthie prodded.

"It's not a sure thing, so don't tell anybody." Natalie cast her a warning glance. But behind it was an excitement she hadn't felt in a long time . . . well, to be honest, maybe never.

"I know how you feel," confessed Ruthie, suddenly sober. "I remember when Stick first brought Sean to youth group. I thought then how terrific he looked—with his great build and that blond hair."

Natalie gave her friend a quizzical look. "What do you mean—*then*? Aren't you two still going together?"

"Sure we are. Hey, maybe Sean and I could double-date with you guys," Ruthie dreamed on. "I'd feel like a princess after riding in Sean's old clunker."

Natalie stopped when they reached Ruthie's house. "Look, he may not even ask me. This may be a trick Cissy is playing."

Ruthie balled up her fist and shook it. "If it is, she'll have to answer to me!"

Natalie laughed, but she had no doubt that tomboyish Ruthie could pack a wallop with that fist if she had a mind to. She appreciated her friend's loyalty. "Really, Ruthie, it doesn't matter all that much. Anyway, Craig and Philip have asked me."

"Who *haven't* they asked?" Ruthie smirked and rolled her eyes. "But you're going to wait for Scott, aren't you?"

Natalie shrugged. "Who knows?"

"Awesome, totally awesome!" Ruthie was saying as Natalie hurried on down the block toward her house, barely registering Natalie's added, "See ya later at church."

At first, everything went as usual at the weekly youth meeting, held in the fellowship hall in the basement of the church. As president, Natalie handled the business session without a hitch, then turned the meeting over to Andy and Stephanie Kelly, the youth leaders, and slid into a seat next to Ruthie at one of the long tables.

Although she was twenty-three, Stephanie looked more like one of the teens in her jeans and with her naturally curly long hair pulled back into a ponytail, Natalie thought. The young woman was always smiling and seemed to glow whenever she looked at Andy. Her husband was a couple of years older than Stephanie, was exceptionally good-looking, and had the kind of personality that kept the youth in line. Natalie thought the couple complemented each other, since Stephanie was so approachable and Andy, more serious-minded.

Instead of the expected Bible study, however, Stephanie produced a plastic grocery sack and took out some small white packages, tied with white satin bows.

Natalie was not surprised when Stick, who had rushed in at the last minute, quipped, "Hey, they finally appreciate us. They're giving us presents!"

When everyone laughed, Stick grinned, too, and glanced at Natalie's sister Amy for approval. She smiled back, and Natalie noticed that his face reddened, tiny beads of sweat glistening on his forehead. That always happened when he was near Amy. Stick was the brunt of a lot of jokes in his outspoken belief that Amy Ainsworth was the prettiest girl in the world.

Natalie understood. In a family of four girls, her sister Amy was the undisputed beauty—golden blond hair, big blue eyes, and skin as clear and soft as a baby's. But Amy was only fourteen, while Stick was sixteen.

"These presents are for you," Andy said after Stephanie finished setting the packages on the table, then folded the bag and laid it aside. She took her seat and looked up at her husband, her eyes shining with love.

"That is, the object inside the box is a symbol of one of the most valuable possessions you'll ever have or can ever give someone else," he went on seriously.

All the whispers and scuffling of feet ceased. What could Andy be talking about? They all knew that the Kellys, who had not been married long, had no extra money. The young couple talked openly about that when they stressed the Bible's teaching on tithing. Many times, they had said, they had no money left over after paying the bills, but they believed God would provide. And He always had. Still, they certainly couldn't afford to give expensive presents.

Andy picked up one of the boxes. "This represents a gift that each of you can give your future mate on your wedding night."

Natalie saw the look of concern that crossed Andy's face when he heard several groans. "Not another lecture on sex!"

But before Andy could utter another word, Billy raised his hand. When Andy acknowledged the thirteen-year-old, the boy cleared his throat, but the words came out kind of squeaky. "My mom and dad said I can't discuss anything like that with anybody—not schoolteachers or . . . anybody!"

There were a few giggles, then Billy's friend piped up, "Mine, too. They don't like some of the school programs on . . . well, they don't even want me talking about . . . you know . . . sex."

The group broke out into nervous laughter. Several began to whisper among themselves.

Natalie and Ruthie exchanged glances. Apparently this was not going to be the usual Bible study session. "Listen to what Andy has to say first," Stephanie urged. "Then we can discuss it."

Gradually, the group quieted down.

"Inside this box," Andy went on, "is a symbol of something that is uniquely your own—your sexuality. It is precious. And very valuable. It seems all we're hearing about today is 'safe sex' and 'being prepared,' as if our religious beliefs no longer play a part in our lives—at least our sex lives."

Andy paused. The room was so still you could hear someone's stomach growl. *Probably Stick's*, Natalie thought. That guy never seemed to get enough to eat, though his weight had not kept up with his height.

"Well, I'm here to tell you that God is still around," Andy continued, "and He has *plenty* to say about our sex lives in His Word. His rules are not intended to deprive us of something good, but to enable us to 'live abundantly,' as Jesus put it. He didn't come to take anything *away* from you, but to *give* you something."

"The reality about sex is not what the world tells us," Stephanie interjected, "but what God's Word tells us."

Andy nodded. "And young people like you all over

the world are beginning to realize that. They're even signing pledge cards, vowing to postpone sex until after marriage."

Glancing around, Natalie could tell that some of her friends were becoming interested. With every word bouncing back and forth between Andy and Stephanie, the program took on more appeal.

"And now the movement has gone worldwide. So"—Andy spread his hands—"what do you think about our joining up?"

"I don't see how it could hurt," said Ruthie with a shrug.

"Sounds okay to me," Amy said, joined by a chorus of approval from her friends.

Taking a lead from Amy, Stick quipped, "Like my grandpa would say, 'Sounds like the greatest thing since sliced bread!'"

As soon as the groans and giggles subsided, Marcie, a petite thirteen-year-old who looked no more than eleven, raised her hand.

"Yes, Marcie?" Andy acknowledged her with a nod.

She swallowed hard, then spoke quietly. "I don't think my parents would approve. They said I'd have to ask *them* if I have any questions about . . . that."

Andy looked concerned but nodded politely.

"My parents discuss sex with me," commented a senior boy, "but they feel I should have all the information I can get, even if they don't agree with all of it. They expect me to use some common sense." He shrugged. "I think they'd go for this program."

Several others said they liked the idea. Some still weren't sure, and some wanted to know more.

"We can't tell you any more without church approval," Andy admitted reluctantly. "I don't expect any opposition, but we do have to take this to your parents, then to the pastor and the Leadership Committee of the church. If they okay it, then we can discuss it further and begin implementing the program at our Wednesday night meetings."

Natalie remained silent. Andy's and Stephanie's examples had taught her that leadership did not mean forcing your views on others, but allowing people to voice their opinions, then making a decision based on the rule of the majority.

After an uncomfortable silence, Lana raised her hand. "I don't think it will work," she said. The group listened because Lana usually made sense.

Natalie knew Andy and Stephanie were surprised at any sign of resistance from the youth group. The couple had come to the church six months ago when youth group attendance was at an all-time low, and had tripled the size of the group by concentrating on a biblical approach to everyday living. No doubt they hoped this program would draw others in during the summer.

Finally Stephanie urged, "You don't have to, Lana, but would you mind telling us why you don't think it will work?"

Lana fidgeted, then swallowed hard before continuing. "Well, not that I intend to do anything, you know, but I'm not sure about signing a card. Doesn't the Bible say it's better not to make a vow to God than to make it and break it?"

"Yeah!" John—the strong, silent type—spoke up, bold now that others were voicing their opinions. "I know some people in this very room who—"

"Hold it!" Andy interrupted. "No one's on trial here. We don't discuss anyone's private life."

John turned suddenly defiant. "Well, did you two wait?"

The big clock on the back wall broke the heavy silence.

"I said we don't—" Andy began, but Stephanie broke in.

"Let me answer that," she said and stood, looking John directly in the eye. "I can answer it easily, because, yes, we did wait. But let's never ask anyone else that question. Imagine how embarrassing it would be if everything you ever said or did was paraded in front of others."

A red flush crept up John's neck and into his face, and he sat down.

Stephanie smiled. "As the Bible says, 'We have all sinned and come short of the glory of God.' And a wonderful part of this program is that a person who has not been sexually pure can ask God's forgiveness, and He will forgive—erase the slate as if the sin never happened! Then that person can start over, vowing to live a sexually pure life from that moment on."

John nodded and the tension in the room seemed to ease.

"Remember," Andy added when Stephanie took her seat again, "Jesus said He came not to condemn people, but to save. So let's make that our goal. Let's not probe and pry, but let's focus on helping one another keep our bodies and minds clean and pure."

"Do you want us to take one of those boxes?" Stick asked.

Andy shook his head. "Not yet. I want you to discuss this among yourselves first. Think about it. Pray about it. Think about what you want to do with your sexuality. About what you would like your future mate to do. Then, after we've brought this idea before the church leaders, we'll let you know if we're going forward with the program."

In the silence that followed, Andy paused, scanning the group. "Stick, come up here, please."

Stick sauntered to the front of the room, beads of sweat popping out on his forehead.

Andy held out one of the boxes. Stick's eyes grew wide, and he jumped back as if the box were a rattlesnake about to strike.

There were a few scattered giggles.

Andy laughed softly. "All I want you to do is throw this box in that trash can."

"In the . . . trash can?" Stick echoed, as if he hadn't heard correctly. "From here?"

"From there. It's only about ten feet away. You've made longer shots on the basketball court."

The giggles swelled to a roar of laughter.

Stick shrugged and looked down at the clean, white package. He took it from Andy, and when he shook it, it rattled. There really was something inside. He lifted his arm and drew it back, then glanced at Andy, as if unsure.

Andy nodded.

Stick tossed the package. It made a perfect arc as it sailed through the air before landing with a thud in the bottom of the can.

"So, think about it," said Andy. "Do you want to

try this program?" He picked up a white box. "Or shall we toss these symbols of your sexuality into the trash can—as if they're no more important than a sack of garbage?"

Two

Siiiiiooooguhhhhh!
Siiiiiooooguhhhhh!
Siiiiiooooguhhhhh!

The tornado alarm system pierced the air with a shrill, ear-splitting noise. The principal himself had described the sound as that of an old Model T's "chi-oo-gah" car horn inside an oil drum—only a hundred times louder.

Immediately, the students threw down their pencils, jumped up from their desks, and filed out of the room, shuffling robotlike—row by row, not speaking except for a few groans and grumbles.

Natalie had been subjected to this kind of drill since kindergarten, but she still got goosebumps every time she heard it, and her heart pounded against her chest with the force of a hammer driving a nail into a two-by-four.

Upon reaching the hallway, each student hurried to a pre-assigned spot. One by one, like dominoes toppling over, they fell to their knees, scooted their bottoms down to their heels, and bent over till their thighs cradled their stomachs and their foreheads touched the

23

floor. Then they clasped their hands at the back of their necks and waited.

Was this the real thing this time? Or was it just another practice drill? Was the roof going to fall in on them? Would they be blown away?

It wasn't so scary on a clear day, but the sky had been cloudy all morning and the winds strong. The only way Natalie knew to calm her erratic heartbeat was to pray. She was sure others were doing the same because no one was making wisecracks—not even Stick.

The worst part, Natalie thought, other than the possibility of being in an actual tornado, was having to assume the humiliating position of placing your head against the backside of the person in front of you, with someone else's skull crammed against yours! Everyone complained about it, but it was supposed to be the safest position.

The alarm trailed off, and the principal announced that the drill was over. But the ringing in the ears wasn't! All at once, the students were getting to their feet and filing back into the classrooms.

"This is what we get for living in Tornado Alley," Ruthie complained, referring to the nickname given to that part of southern Illinois as she slid into her seat.

Natalie tried to look at the positive side. During her lifetime, a tornado had never struck Garden City, although several had touched down in the surrounding countryside. There were threats and warnings every year, of course, especially in the spring and fall. "At least it was just a drill." She gestured toward the clock. "And the bell's going to ring any minute."

"But I still don't understand that last algebra problem." Ruthie's face took on a worried look, unlike her usual sunny countenance. "I'm never going to pass algebra. Maybe we'll have a tornado drill during the exam and someone can tell me the answers."

"Wouldn't help," Natalie countered, gathering up her books. "You know the teacher wants us to show our work so she can see if we know how to solve the problems."

When the bell rang, both girls jumped. Laughing nervously, they grabbed their stuff and hurried out of the classroom.

"We could study together if you like," Natalie offered on the way to their lockers.

Ruthie grinned weakly. "Maybe that would help. I don't know a 'cute' angle from an 'abuse' one."

"Obtuse," Natalie corrected.

"See!" Ruthie spread her hands in exasperation.

Natalie laughed in spite of herself, not at her friend's predicament, but at her antics. Ruthie could get so uptight—almost as tight as the bright red ringlets that sprang all over her head. "You're really clever with words. And you make straight A's in English. So don't be so down on yourself."

Ruthie smiled, but her eyes were clouded with doubt.

———

On the way home from school, beneath a threatening sky, the feel of a brisk wind against their faces, Ruthie spoke up. "I'm going to have to cram. When could we study together?"

Natalie's mom had a class at the junior college on Monday and Thursday nights, and her dad was on the evening shift at the federal prison this quarter, with Tuesdays and Wednesdays off. "My parents won't be home tonight, so this is not a good time."

"Oh, and both my parents are going to that special meeting about the youth abstinence program *tomorrow* night," Ruthie remembered. "I'll have to stay home with Justin." She made a face and wrinkled her nose. "You know what a 'wholly terror' he is. That's spelled w-h-o-l-l-y, and I do mean *completely!*"

Natalie laughed. "It couldn't be any worse than my house. Amy is usually practicing her cheers, Sarah's hitting the side of the house with her basketball, and Rose is marching through the house playing the kazoo. Meanwhile, someone leaves the TV on, the phone rings—"

"I thought you had such a peaceful household."

"That *is* peaceful," Natalie agreed with a grin. "You should see us on the days we argue!"

Ruthie grinned back, then recalling something Andy had said at the meeting, turned down her lips and placed her hands over her heart. "Oh, and on Wednesday, we must . . . take a bath!"

"Yeah," Natalie mused, quirking her brow. "Imagine Andy telling us to bathe and change into clean clothes before coming to the youth group meeting."

"I usually keep on what I wore to school that day."

"Me too. But Stephanie explained that she and Andy want us to be clean for a reason."

Ruthie nodded. "I'll bet I know why. It's got something to do with looking as clean and perfect as those little white packages."

"I suppose so. Wonder what's in them?"

"They'll tell us soon, I guess. Andy said it's just a formality getting parent and church leader approval before he can give us the details on the program."

Natalie nodded, her blue eyes appearing almost gray as they reflected the overcast sky. "I keep thinking of that package in the trash can. There are too many people who treat sex like garbage. Sometimes at a movie, I think, 'Boy, I'm glad I'm not seeing this with a guy.'"

Ruthie turned to look at her friend. "Speaking of guys . . . any more news about Scott Lambert?"

"None," Natalie replied, trying not to sound disappointed. "Cissy just said he *might* ask me, you know."

"Well, it's still early. The prom is two weeks away."

They walked on in silence. Natalie had tried to resign herself to the fact that Scott probably wouldn't ask her. But when she turned onto the walkway leading up to the brick house where she lived, she saw Amy stepping out onto the porch.

Amy grabbed the white column and swung forward, calling out, "Telephone, Nat!"

"Who is it?"

Amy shrugged. "Some boy."

Probably Craig or Philip, Natalie told herself, hoping it wasn't. Then, she hoped it was because she'd be tongue-tied if it was . . . someone else!

"Natalie?" The voice on the other end of the line was one she had never heard on the phone before— deep and serious and very nice.

"Yes?" she answered, breathless from having hurried into the house. At least that was the excuse she gave herself.

"Scott Lambert here. You probably don't know me. . . ."

On the tip of her tongue was, "Oh, everyone knows you, especially all the girls!" But she resisted uttering the ridiculous remark. "Yes," she replied instead, "I've seen you around. You . . . uh . . . run track, don't you? And you're Cissy's . . . uh . . . cousin."

She could kick herself! She must sound like a real dork!

"Right."

He sounded relieved. Maybe he thought she was a friend of Cissy's. Maybe he didn't know how ordinary she was.

"If you don't have any plans, would you like to go out with me on Saturday night?"

Are you kidding? Natalie kept that thought to herself but managed to ask, "What did you have in mind?"

"Well, I checked and there aren't any decent movies showing, but . . ."

Good, he likes "decent movies." That's a plus.

" . . . there's a play at the university at Carbondale. Does that interest you?"

"I *love* plays!" Natalie gushed, realizing that most of the ones she had seen had been put on by the drama department at school. That wasn't lying, was it?

"It's a mystery comedy called *Who Killed the Butler?*"

"At least we know the butler didn't do it," she said with a chuckle.

"Not necessarily," he returned. "The butler could have done himself in."

Pleased with his perceptive retort, Natalie thought fast. "True, and that just adds to the suspense." Then she added quickly, "I'll have to clear it with my parents. Dad's at work and Mom's at the grocery store."

"Great. I'll call later in the week to see if we're on."

Cool! she thought as she thanked him and hung up. "Awesome!" she squealed, dancing around the living room. Normally, she tried for more creative speech, disdaining the stock phrases that rolled out automatically from Amy and Ruthie and most of the other people her age. But this was not a normal situation, and *awesome* was the only word that fit.

"What in the world brought that on?" asked Jill Ainsworth, coming in the house with a load of groceries. "Did you win a vacation to Hawaii or something?"

"Oh, better than that, Mom! The neatest guy has asked me out." Seeing that her mother didn't appear overly impressed, Natalie added, "He seems more . . . mature than most."

"I think you'd better come with me into the kitchen so we can discuss this, young lady," her mother said in no uncertain terms. "I have supper to fix before I leave for class."

"Oh, I could have done that," Natalie said cheerfully.

"Since when? You hate to cook."

"Not tonight," she said in a lilting tone.

Her mother gave her a searching look. "I have this strange feeling that if you cooked tonight, everything would be very crisp!" she kidded after peeking into the oven to check on the chicken. "Now tell me about this dreamboat."

29

Natalie told her all she knew.

"You know that's not enough information, honey. We have to know something about his parents, what kind of background he comes from . . ."

"Oh, Mom, really! Are you afraid he'll turn out to be from the wrong side of the tracks?"

Her mother shook her head. "It's not that. It's just that you've only been out with groups of friends and boys we've known all our lives. This is different, isn't it?"

Natalie felt her excitement beginning to wane. She lowered her eyes from her mother's knowing gaze. Yes, this *was* different. It was like a first real date. With someone who could be . . . more than a friend.

"Find out what you can about him," her mom said with a sense of finality. "Then your father and I will sit down and talk it over with you."

Natalie could see a huge imaginary bubble floating precariously through the air. She forced herself to stop thinking about it before it popped.

———

With things so uncertain, Natalie didn't tell Ruthie or anyone that Scott had called. Instead, after school, she went to her small attic hideaway over the garage and tried to study. When sharing a room with Amy-the-cheerleader had gotten to be too much, her dad had suggested this alternative. The slant of the walls meant she could only stand up in the center of the room, but as she told her dad, "I intend to *lie* on the bed and *sit* at the desk anyway—not stand on them."

She loved it. The cream-and-blue decor suited her.

Best of all, she had some privacy!

After a short while, Natalie went down to help with supper, eager to get it on the table so there would be time to discuss her "possible date" before her dad left for the meeting at church. Her mom wouldn't be going.

"I don't want to leave you in charge two nights in a row, Natalie," Jill explained after the family, holding hands, had finished praying. "Your dad and I feel pretty much the same about things, so he can represent us both at the meeting."

"This is a busy week for me, Mom," Natalie acknowledged as she helped herself to one of the individual pot pies her mom had made using last night's leftover baked chicken. "Tomorrow night is youth group and . . ." She looked at her mom with a sly grin.

"And?" her mother asked innocently, as if this were any old week at all.

"And," Natalie went along with the game, "I have to study for finals."

"You don't expect any trouble there, do you?" her dad asked. "You're a good student." He slid a forkful of pie into his mouth.

"She's *smart*," Amy remarked, excusing her own B and C average.

Natalie glanced at her younger sister. "I *study*."

"Meaning I don't?" Amy shot back defensively.

"Now, girls—" their dad began.

"I'm just saying that if I'm smart, it's because I study," Natalie insisted. "Information doesn't just float down from the sky and lodge in my brain, you know."

"Wait a minute," Jill cautioned, "this conversation is getting out of hand. I've warned you girls about comparing. Each one of you is special in your own way. You're not engaged in a competition. Now, we have a very important matter to discuss with your father."

Natalie felt her cheeks grow warm. This was it. She'd soon know if her dad would let her go out with Scott Lambert.

Jim Ainsworth took a gulp of iced tea, then set his glass down. "What's up?"

"Oh, I just wondered what you wanted for dinner tomorrow night, dear," her mother teased.

Natalie's heart did a somersault, then plunged into her stomach. "Mo-om!" This was no time for games. A life-changing decision was at stake.

"Okay, okay," Jill said, turning a serious look on Jim. "Our daughter has been asked out by a boy who is . . . absolutely groovy."

"Mom," Natalie corrected, "nobody's groovy anymore."

"Fantastic?"

Natalie grinned.

"And he has a cranberry sports car," Jill continued.

"But, of course," Natalie said playfully, deepening her voice and drawing her brows together as her dad often did, "who cares if he's wearing roller skates? The important thing is if his heart's in the right place." Her dad always said things like that. She knew he meant, "Is this guy a Christian?"

"Well?" Jim waited, peering over his glasses while Natalie's younger sisters giggled. "*Is* his heart in the right place? How old is he? And does this 'real date' have a name?"

When Natalie replied, "Scott Lambert," Amy came as unglued as Ruthie had earlier, and Natalie shot her a warning glance. Dad wouldn't like it if he thought she judged a boy's character on the basis of something as superficial as his looks or the kind of car he drove.

Natalie had to admit she didn't know much about Scott. Only that he had moved to town this past year and had started his junior year at Shawnee High.

Her dad had "no" written all over his face until Natalie added quickly, "But he's a cousin of Cissy Stiles, the niece of Mrs. Brysen at our church."

Jim's dark eyes sparked with recognition. "Oh yes. Dr. Lawrence Lambert. He's on the staff at the hospital here." He glanced at his wife. "He married one of Martha Brysen's sisters." He seemed ready to say more, then sent Jill an "I'll-tell-you-later" look. "This . . . Scott . . . wants to take you to a play?" he asked Natalie.

She shrugged. "He said there was no decent movie playing."

"Decent, huh?" Jim's eyebrows lifted slightly. "What's the play?"

"*Who Killed the Butler?*"

"Well, why see it? You already know the butler didn't do it." Her dad threw back his head and laughed heartily at his own joke.

"Not really," Natalie returned. "The butler could have killed himself."

"Ah!" Her dad seemed pleasantly surprised. "That's very clever, Natalie."

She grinned. "I thought so, too . . . when Scott told me."

"Hmmm. He sounds like an intelligent young man."

Natalie glanced at Amy, who was watching their father with great anticipation, as if his decision would change her life forever. Natalie tried to mask her own flyaway emotions, but when she looked down at her lap, she realized she was about to twist her fingers off!

An eternity passed while Jim studied his plate with a thoughtful expression. Finally his eyes met Natalie's. "I think it might be all right."

"So that's a yes?" Amy pressed.

"Not for you, young lady! You're only fourteen."

"Oh, will time ever stop crawling?" Amy groaned. "Two more years before I can get a car like that. Or"—she turned a mischievous grin on Natalie—"a hunk who drives one."

"Amy," her mother cautioned, "boys aren't hunks, they're people. Now, it's your turn to serve dessert."

Amy sighed, relinquishing her fantasy. "Everyone want some?" She looked around the table and focused on Natalie, who knew what that smug look on her sister's face meant. If Natalie said no to dessert, then she'd be accused of being in love.

"Amy," she said with mock sweetness, "I could never turn down Mom's Texas sheet cake."

Natalie was sitting at her desk poring over a reading assignment when Amy rushed into the room.

"Don't you ever knock?" Natalie complained, swiveling her chair around to face her sister.

"I did!"

"The idea is to knock first, wait to be invited in, then enter. Not knock as you burst through the doorway."

"Sorry! I'll remember next time." Amy plopped down onto the bed, grabbed a decorative pillow, then propped her forearms on it. "Whatcha gonna wear Saturday night?"

Natalie could never stay mad at her lively sister for long. But Amy's exuberance was one reason Natalie needed her own space. "Haven't decided."

Amy jumped up.

"You do that in here, and you'll bump your head," Natalie warned.

"Oooops!" Amy scrunched over to the closet. "You have absolutely nothing to wear on an important date. You'll have to borrow one of Mom's outfits."

"I've got plenty of my own," Natalie protested. "My Easter suit, skirts and blouses . . ."

"Oh, Nat, this is special. Scott Lambert is not just *any* guy."

"I was wearing my rattiest jeans when he asked me out, so it really doesn't matter."

Amy shook her head. "You're hopeless, Nat. You really need me on this one. I'll make a list—lip gloss, fingernail polish the color of his car, Mom's dangly earrings . . ."

Natalie laughed. The image of being made up for Halloween flashed through her mind. "Make your list, sis, and I'll see what I can do."

Aware of how close she felt to her younger sister, she smiled and wandered over to her closet as Amy left the room. "What *am* I going to wear?" she wondered aloud.

It was after ten o'clock when Jim Ainsworth returned from the church. Even though the meeting had not been expected to last long, more than two hours had passed before Natalie heard his knock on her bedroom door.

"Come in," she called.

He opened the door, looked in, then entered to sit on the edge of her bed. "The meeting didn't go at all as I expected, Natalie," he said with a somewhat bewildered expression on his face. "Andy's presentation of the abstinence program was impressive. I think the idea would be an excellent one for our youth group, but . . ."

Natalie stared at him. Why was her father having difficulty telling her what had happened? He always spoke his mind.

"There were a lot of questions, but most of the parents were in favor of giving it a try"—he paused—"until one person expressed her strong feelings in opposition. Then some began having second thoughts."

Natalie was genuinely puzzled. "Who was against it, Dad?"

"Your new friend's aunt . . . Martha Brysen." At the troubled look on Natalie's face, he hurried on, "But just because Mrs. Brysen and I disagree about the abstinence program is no reason for me to go back on my word about your date with Scott."

As for the woman's reasons for disliking the program, her dad wouldn't say. He probably didn't want her to think the church was divided on the issue, Natalie guessed.

"We all have the best interests of the youth group at heart," he said seriously. "The thing to do now is pray."

After he left the room and Natalie had snapped off the bedside lamp, she looked toward the window where the soft moonlight filtered in. *Dear God*, she prayed, *please help the youth group to get along, and keep Andy and Stephanie from becoming discouraged.*

Three

"Sorry you had to wash up for no reason," Andy teased, glancing around the room at the scrubbed faces and still-damp hair of the youth group as they settled in for the Wednesday night meeting.

There was a chorus of groans.

"At least," Stick piped up, "I won't have to take my usual Saturday night bath."

"Oh, gross, Stick!" Amy exclaimed, wrinkling her nose.

"She spoke to me. She actually spoke to me!" He jabbed his friend Brad in the arm.

Amy's long blond ponytail bounced as she turned her back on Stick and began talking with one of her own friends.

"Okay, let's get down to business about this abstinence program," Andy said, relating some of the same things Natalie's dad had told her. "Since the parents had so many questions and since there was some disagreement among them, the pastor felt the church leaders should make the final decision."

To Natalie's surprise, Andy turned to her. "As president of the youth group, Natalie," he said, "you should be our representative at that meeting."

"B-but I can't speak for everyone else," she protested.

Andy's and Stephanie's faces reflected their own frustration. "I know, but we won't be able to show the videos and discuss the content of the program with the youth group until after it's approved by the leaders."

Natalie swallowed hard. How could this be God's answer to her prayer? "But I don't know anything about the program."

Andy smiled. "The parents decided that the youth representative should view the materials and see the video."

Natalie remembered her dad's pensive look and the seriousness of his tone as they had talked. He must have had an idea that she would be chosen to represent the youth group.

But . . . if the *parents* couldn't decide, how could *she* be expected to do any better? Well, she didn't intend to go out on a limb all by herself. "Could we take a vote first to see how much interest there is in the program?" she asked cautiously.

"Sure we could," Stephanie spoke up. "Basically, it's about purity of lifestyle, but it includes young people agreeing not to have sex until they're married. The program discusses the reasons, and the participants vow to remain sexually pure."

With such a sensitive issue, they decided to vote by secret ballot.

Afterward, Stephanie gathered the votes and Andy tallied them, then reported: "Five—'not sure'; seven—'no'; eighteen—'yes.'"

"How do we know you counted right?" Billy demanded.

When almost everyone began jumping down Billy's throat, he held up his hands in mock surrender. "Hey, you guys, I was only kidding. Can't anyone take a joke around here?"

Andy waited patiently until they had settled down, then continued. "At the meeting last night, I heard opposition from some very fine people who have been Christians longer than I've been living. Now I'm glad the ultimate decision will be made by the leaders."

"Then we might not ever know what's in those little packages?" Amy asked, still curious.

"If he lets me toss them all into the trash can," Stick pitched in, "I'll save one for you and we'll see."

"Never mind," she moaned.

The silly grin was plastered all over Stick's face once again.

"Do we have to shower next Wednesday, too?" Ruthie asked playfully.

Andy laughed. "The church leaders meet Sunday afternoon. If the vote is in favor, I'll appoint a telephone committee. Wouldn't want anyone to clean up unnecessarily."

"Would it count if I just stood out in the rain?" asked Stick with an eye on Amy to see if she was listening.

She sighed heavily, weary of his attempts to impress her. "Even a high wind wouldn't blow away *that* locker-room smell!" She pinched her nostrils between her thumb and forefinger.

"Thanks, Amy," Stick said, still smiling. Everyone

knew he didn't care what Amy Ainsworth said as long as she was speaking to him.

Natalie felt sorry for Stick. He was crazy about her adorable sister. Strange that it had never seemed to occur to him that with the difference in their ages, by the time Amy was allowed to date, he'd be out of high school. She would *still* be off limits.

But that was the least of Natalie's worries at the moment. She was really nervous about the meeting coming up on Sunday. And before that, she'd be going out with Scott. Did he know about his aunt's opposition to the abstinence program? Would he, too, be against it?

———

Am I going out with Scott for the wrong reasons? Natalie asked herself on Thursday morning before the day was barely underway. She really didn't know a thing about him other than that he was good-looking. Was he even a Christian? Natalie sighed. She wasn't always consistent about living as a Christian should. *For that matter, who is?* she comforted herself.

Still, her faith hadn't ever really been tested. And now with the prospect of going to the prom with the "mystery man" in school—the one with the neat sports car—she wondered if she could keep her priorities straight. At the thought of Scott, Natalie's heartbeat sped up—just as it had been doing ever since his call last night to confirm their date.

Now, sitting in English class writing out answers to a reading assignment, she felt the uneasy sensation that someone was watching her. Glancing up, she met Mrs.

Johnson's puzzled gaze. Across the aisle, Ruthie snickered into her hand.

It was only then that Natalie realized she'd been humming out loud! "Sorry," she mouthed to the teacher, who smiled and nodded.

Feeling her face growing red, Natalie ducked her head and bit her lip. Actually, she'd unconsciously been reveling in thoughts of Scott Lambert. *Saturday night will be my* first *big date!* She hugged herself, then added on a more solemn note, *But if I let my grades slide, it may be my* last *date!*

Though Natalie had never thought of herself as shy or self-conscious, when she got to study hall, she chose a front table with her back to the rest of the room so she wouldn't be facing Scott. Normally, that table was empty, being in full view of the school librarian, who was strict about maintaining complete silence in the library.

To her surprise, Stick, who did not have study hall this period, came in before the bell rang and handed her a note. On his way out, he bumped against a table, then backed into a girl with an armload of books. He mumbled his apologies.

Natalie unfolded the paper. The letters were smudged, almost as if the paper had been damp when he wrote: "Do you think Amy (would, might, could) go to the prom with me?"

It really wasn't funny, but Natalie couldn't help smiling. Stick had written those words and then crossed them out before scribbling, "Do you think there's a chance she'd go?" *He even stutters on paper, just thinking of Amy.*

Soon Natalie began to suspect that taking a seat at the front table had been the worst thing she could have done. She was so conspicuous sitting there all alone. But when Marla and two of her closest friends came in and joined her, Natalie drew a sigh of relief. Not for long. The other three girls began whispering and writing notes about Scott.

The whole school must be talking about her date! She had told Ruthie and Amy not to tell anyone except one close friend. Probably those close friends had told only "one close friend," which meant that by now the entire student body knew her business.

After school, Stick ran up to her, eager to know her answer to his question. Before she could reply, he added, "Hey, we could double-date with you two, couldn't we?"

She certainly didn't want her younger sister and Stick tagging along with her and Scott to the prom—*if* he asked her, that is. Besides, she wasn't sure her parents would allow Amy to attend, even if it was a group function. Well, it was a moot point anyway. Amy would never go *anywhere* with Stick Gordon.

Natalie shrugged. "I can't answer for Amy or my parents," was all she could tell him. She felt a little twinge of remorse when she left him looking downcast.

When she and Ruthie walked out the front door, even the stiff breeze couldn't blow away Natalie's euphoria. She felt a kinship with Tecumseh, who didn't flinch, either, as the wind whipped around his cement base.

"Here comes trouble!" said Ruthie loudly just as Natalie spotted Katlyn Chander moving out of the shadows, where she was apparently shielding herself from the wind.

Katlyn either didn't hear or she didn't care what Ruthie had just said. There had been bad blood between them since last year when Katlyn had beaten Ruthie out of a leading role in one of the drama productions, and Ruthie had been given a small part. Since that time, Katlyn had treated Ruthie like a second-class citizen—both on and off the stage.

Ignoring Ruthie, Katlyn pushed her long black hair away from her face and smiled coldly. "Congratulations, Natalie."

"Oh, thanks! But what did I do?"

"I hear you've got a date with Scott Lambert."

"Where'd you hear that?"

"Oh, come on. Everyone knows. I just wanted to warn you: Scott never dates a girl more than once."

Katlyn's eyes narrowed and Natalie couldn't help thinking that, at that moment, the dark-haired girl really did resemble a cat! Her insight was confirmed when she felt Ruthie's fingernails digging into her back and heard a small "Meow" from behind her. Natalie laughed. "Thanks, Katlyn. I'll remember that."

"Just thought I'd let you know." The tall girl strolled away as gracefully as one could manage in a high wind.

Ruthie gave a disapproving snort. "Well, *her* claws were showing."

"But why?" Natalie was mystified. "Why would Katlyn, who never bothers to speak unless absolutely necessary, make a special point of it?"

"Isn't it obvious? She's jealous."

"Come on. She's got everything."

Ruthie grinned. "Yeah, everything—except Scott!"

Natalie grinned back. But she felt as if some of the wind had been knocked out of her. Worse than that, she had to admit she really didn't like Katlyn. It was not a good feeling.

———————

Natalie went to bed thinking about her date. It was still on her mind the next morning when she awoke.

Apparently, she wasn't the only one. At breakfast, Amy spoke first. "Well, this is *it*!"

"What's 'it'?" Sarah asked, peering sleepily through her tousled mop of sable brown hair.

"Natalie's date with Scott tonight," Amy mumbled through a mouthful of cereal.

"Oh," Sarah said with the unconcern of a twelve-year-old. She was going through what Jill called an I-hate-boys-soon-to-be-an-I-love-boys-so-watch-out stage. "Dad, I want a gerbil."

He peeked over his newspaper. "You can't have a gerbil."

"Why not?"

He turned a page. "We don't have much luck with those animals. They always die," he said through the sports section.

"I want a live one."

"You already have an aquarium in your room."

"Yeah, but I share that with Rose. Besides, she has a puppy, too."

Ten-year-old Rose was the one child in the family who never seemed to get perturbed about anything. At the mention of her dog, clear blue eyes lit up her sweet, angelic face. "He's the most beautiful puppy in the world. I named him Pongo because he has spots like Pongo in *101 Dalmatians*," she explained for the umpteenth time.

"He's not a *real* Dalmatian," Sarah reminded her a little unkindly. "Remember? Dad got him from the pound."

Rose's left cheek dimpled as she smiled. "But I love him anyway."

"Everyone has something but *me*," Sarah fumed.

"What have *I* got?" Amy asked cheerfully.

Sarah rolled her eyes. "Cheerleading and booooooys."

"What's Natalie got?"

"Scott," Sarah stated matter-of-factly before turning again to her dad. "Couldn't I at least have one little gerbil?"

He lowered his paper enough to peer at her over his glasses. "Ask your mother."

"Are you excited, Nat?" Amy interrupted.

"Mmmm. A little," she hedged.

Just then, Rose slipped her a handmade card. On the front her youngest sister had drawn stick figures of a boy and girl. With watercolors, she had painted a dress on one and shirt and pants on the other. In the background was a red car. The edges were stylized splotches of pink, purple, and green. And inside, was a hand-lettered message:

Violets are purple—
Roses are pink.
You're the greatest—
That's what I think.

Underneath was a personal note: "Have a great date! Love from me and kisses from you-know-who." In the corner she had drawn a tiny rose.

Natalie stared at the card. Her youngest sister often created her own special-occasion greeting cards—Christmas, Valentine's Day, birthdays, get-well wishes.

"You like it?" Rose asked in a small voice.

"Of course I like it. I was just thinking how talented and special you are." She gave her little sister a hug and tapped on the paper. "Dad, look at this."

He crumpled his paper once more and looked up. "Now what?" When he saw the card, he put down his paper to examine it. "That's really good, baby. Go show your mother."

Shyly, Rose carried the card into the living room, where Jill Ainsworth was exercising to a TV aerobics program.

One by one, the other girls finished their breakfast and left the kitchen. Only Natalie and her dad were left sitting there.

"Would you pour me some more coffee, honey?"

"Sure, Dad." She got up, brought the carafe from the kitchen counter, and refilled his cup.

He lowered his paper and winked. "Thanks. And by the way, have a good time tonight."

Supper that evening was Natalie's favorite—ham

and macaroni and cheese. Her mom had even fixed asparagus, which was *no* one else's favorite. To make up for it, there was a bowl of tiny green peas for the other three girls.

"You can use my bathroom, Natalie." Her mom gave her an understanding smile. "Why don't you take a long, luxurious bubble bath?"

"Thanks, Mom," she said but opted for a shower. Normally, she shared a bathroom with her three sisters and was never able to finish without someone pounding on the door demanding she hurry.

"Can she wear that perfume Dad gave you for your birthday, Mom?" Amy asked excitedly.

"I don't need all that stuff," Natalie protested, growing more self-conscious by the second.

"A little dab wouldn't hurt," her mom said, making Natalie wonder if maybe she did need it.

After her shower and shampoo, Natalie sat at her dressing table. Amy had insisted on blow-drying her hair and styling it. Natalie went along good-naturedly, while Sarah and Rose perched on the bed, watching every move. But she drew the line when Amy experimented with a glamorous style, and allowed her sister only to fluff out a few strands of hair on either side of her face so her little pearl earrings would show.

"You're gorgeous!" Amy gushed as they studied Natalie's reflection in the mirror.

She had to admit she did look pretty good. Just a touch of eye shadow had made her deep-blue eyes sparkle—or "something" had! She had been told she was pretty, but with her sister's face so near, Natalie could clearly see who was the real beauty. Even with no makeup and hair straggling out of her ponytail, Amy was a knockout.

"Are your sisters bothering you?" her mother asked, peering into the room.

"They're . . . helping." Natalie flashed her mother a skeptical look, softened by a smile. "But I *would* like to get dressed by myself."

Her mom motioned to her sisters, and they reluctantly paraded out of the room. Natalie sighed, watching them go. With all this ruckus over a simple date, what in the world would her family do if she did go to the prom with Scott? Sure, she was glad they cared. But a girl needed *some* privacy.

As soon as she was alone, though, little butterflies began acting up in her stomach—growing bigger by the minute. Because of her excitement, Natalie hadn't eaten as much supper as usual. Amy had told her she'd better eat, or her stomach would growl at the wrong moment. Natalie knew she was right. It always happened at church. *Oh, please don't let it happen tonight!*

Natalie was ready ten minutes early. Her sandals barely touched the ground as she came down the stairs to the hallway. Her family—everyone but her dad, who was at work—was waiting for her in the living room.

"You look beautiful," Rose and Sarah said in unison, while Amy gave a thumbs up. Her mom nodded approvingly.

"Thanks," Natalie said but felt compelled to add, "but this is just a simple little date."

"Oh no, it's not!" Amy protested. "Not with a hunk like Scott and a cranberry sports car."

"My little girl is growing up," her mother said, a

sheen of tears in her eyes. "You look so pretty, honey."

Natalie pushed up the sleeves of her ivory waist-length jacket. She had left it unbuttoned so the blouse would show—a light shade of blue to enhance her eyes. She'd been told her eyes were her best feature. The short skirt matched her jacket.

"This was my Easter outfit, remember?" Natalie reminded the girls, who were gaping as if they'd never seen her before.

"Vaguely," Jill agreed. "But you know how hectic our Sunday mornings are. No one has time to notice anyone else—even on Easter."

Yes, Natalie did know. Invariably, something went wrong on Sunday mornings. The dress Sarah had intended to wear was crumpled on the closet floor . . . or Rose's skirt had a stain on it. And someone was always having a bad hair day. It was a wonder they ever made it to church!

Things had calmed down a little now that Natalie had her own room. At least she could escape some of the hullabaloo, although it was her Sunday-morning duty to help with the younger girls.

Now they were all staring at her as if she were Cinderella on her way to the ball. She returned their approving smiles—until she heard a car door slam outside. Then she bit her lip, feeling herself grow pale.

Amy hurried to the front window with Sarah and Rose right behind her. "There he is!" Amy announced excitedly. "Look, Mom! Didn't I tell you he was a hunk?"

"Amy . . ." her mother warned as she walked toward the front door.

"Let me, Mom," Natalie pleaded.

Jill obliged but not before stealing a peek out the side window. "Why, he's a doll."

Natalie had time for only a quick roll of her eyes and a grin at her mother before Scott was on the doorstep. Natalie opened the door even before he'd had time to ring the bell.

"Hi," they said in unison.

As she opened the door wider, Natalie heard the racing of feet, followed by a *swoosh*—her three sisters, no doubt, flopping onto the couch and a nearby chair.

"Come in," Natalie said, stepping aside so Scott could enter. His large frame filled the door opening. She noticed how nice he looked in casual dress pants and a short-sleeved knit shirt.

"This is my family." She turned to see her sisters sitting demurely around the living room. Her mother was standing with her hands folded in front of her, beaming.

Natalie wished she had asked the girls to stay out of sight. Now she had no choice but to introduce them. "This is Scott Lambert," she began, then gestured toward her mother. "My mother, Jill Ainsworth." She'd barely gotten the words out of her mouth when Scott moved forward to shake Jill's hand.

Taking the initiative, he approached Amy. Obviously enamored, she shook his hand vigorously. Then Sarah, whose main interest in boys was to learn what sport they played, gave him a nonchalant wave. Rose looked adorably shy as color crept into her cheeks, and she peered up at Scott with questioning blue eyes.

Observing the ease with which Scott had greeted

her family, Natalie figured he must have passed the acid test dozens of times.

After he'd met all her sisters, Jill explained that Natalie's dad was working on the second shift at the prison.

Scott perked up. "There's a man who lives in Garden Acres who works at the prison," he replied courteously. "John Kemp, I believe."

"Oh yes, we know the Kemps," Jill replied. "So, you live in Garden Acres."

"Yes."

For the first time, Natalie thought Scott seemed a little uncomfortable. Maybe it was because Garden Acres was so ritzy.

Her mother must have noticed it, too, because she filled the awkward silence immediately. "Don't let us keep you. We wouldn't want you to be late for the play, would we, girls?"

After goodbyes all around, Scott held the door open for Natalie, then escorted her to the car. *He sure is polite*, she thought with a delicious little shiver. Was this really happening?

When he walked around to slide behind the wheel, Natalie glanced back at the house. Sure enough, several heads could be seen peering around one side of the front window. Her mom, however, stood boldly at the front door. "Have a good time," Jill called out. "Be careful."

Scott fastened his seat belt and turned the key in the ignition. The engine started smoothly. He glanced over at Natalie and smiled.

She smiled back, then stared blankly at the street in front of them. It was as if she had never seen it before in her life. Normally, communication was no problem, but right now she couldn't think of a thing to say!

Four

Natalie's earlier concern soon proved groundless. Scott kept the conversation going. He seemed particularly interested in her dad's job at the federal prison.

"Is it hard to adjust to his working different hours every three months?" Scott asked after her brief explanation.

Natalie shrugged. "We're used to it. And he likes the variety—morning shift, evening shift, overnights. He's a senior officer specialist, which means he sometimes supervises the mail room, clothing room, dining room, kitchen, the infirmary, shops. And sometimes he works the control center."

"What kind of controls?"

"Oh, you know. You've probably seen those TV cop shows where one guy sits in front of a bunch of TVs so he can watch the various parts of the prison. He's the one who makes sure everyone is properly identified before opening and closing steel and barred doors. Also, he can close off sections if there's trouble or threat of a riot."

Scott slanted her a curious look. "Sounds dangerous."

"Most of the time it's not. When he's in the outside tower, he has the advantage, including the weapons. Mom worries about him when he's on outside security during the winter, though, checking fences and gates. But it's not the prisoners she's worried about—it's the weather!"

Scott laughed with her. "He must have to stay in pretty good shape to handle all that."

She cut her eyes over at him. "Especially when he chases escapees."

"You're kidding!"

"Nope. That's part of the job."

"Don't you ever worry about your dad?"

"No," Natalie said, knowing that sounded ironic. "And Mom says it doesn't seem real to her—her nice, gentle husband out chasing hardened criminals. Even Dad says that his work is like an entirely different world. He doesn't talk about it much at home."

Scott sighed. "What a life. My dad's job as a doctor isn't nearly as exciting."

"Do you have any sisters and brothers?"

"My only brother is in his second year at college," he said, and Natalie got the distinct impression that Scott wished he were part of a larger family. "What's it like having three sisters?"

They both laughed when she told him how harried things could get in a family of six.

Time seemed to travel faster than the little red sports car, which had not exceeded the speed limit once on the entire trip to Carbondale. It didn't seem possible that forty-five minutes had passed. However, Scott was turning in at a sign that read: "Southern Illinois University."

Natalie marveled at how well they were getting along, then realized that all the talk had been centered around her family. He had seemed so interested and asked so many questions. She suddenly realized that she didn't know any more about Scott Lambert than when they had left home.

"I want to hear about *your* family on the way back," she suggested. She hoped to steer the conversation around to the prom—to give him a chance to ask her—if he intended to.

"Right now," he said, turning onto the college campus, "let's see if we can find a parking place."

At the university theater, Scott presented the tickets and they were ushered to seats about a third of the way from the front. They were both studying their programs when the lights dimmed. In the hush that followed, Natalie wondered if everyone else could feel the silence like she could.

There had been no problem chatting with Scott in the car with the sound of tires against the road, traffic whizzing by, air rushing against the windshield, and bucket seats separating them. The fact that it had still been broad daylight helped, too.

Now they sat very close together, the rest of the audience fading into the shadows. It gave her the feeling that they were the only two people in the whole room.

She swallowed and hoped he couldn't hear. Oh no! The thought of a stomach growl entered her head. It *would* happen—she just knew it! As a nervous reaction, Natalie put her arm on the armrest. His was already there!

Natalie jerked her arm away and folded her hands

over her program on her lap. He moved his arm, too, and leaned away from her. Maybe he didn't like her mom's perfume!

Fortunately, before her breathing became too audible, the curtain went up, and they joined in the applause. Good! At least now she had something to do with her hands. She turned her head slightly, far enough to see that Scott was staring straight ahead at the stage.

Right away, it was obvious that the play was a spoof set in the English countryside, complete with maid and butler. The lead characters were at odds with each other and, before long, Natalie was laughing at the zany lines, flavored with a thick Cockney accent. The audience roared—until the butler appeared on the kitchen floor, splattered with blood. The laughter ceased and everything grew quiet again.

At this point, the tension mounted, and Natalie couldn't tell what was more responsible for her quickening heartbeat—the suspenseful play . . . or Scott's nearness.

When the curtain went down on Act I, Natalie and Scott followed the audience, streaming out into the lobby toward the concession stand. They had just stepped outside into the cool night air to sip their drinks when Natalie heard a familiar voice call cheerfully, "Hi, kiddos."

Natalie swallowed and licked a trickle of soda from her lips before she could return the greeting. Looking up at the tall vision before her, she really *felt* like a kid.

Cissy's dress resembled a cloud of filmy lavender foam and, when she moved her arms, the sleeves fluttered like tiny wings. The neckline formed a V in front and was fastened with a large purple brooch, outlined in silver, with earrings to match. Strappy sandals with high heels completed the perfect picture.

"This is Ron," Cissy said, introducing the dark-haired, good-looking guy who stood beside her with a possessive arm around her waist. "He's a sophomore here."

Cissy seemed quite proud of that fact, and Ron was looking at her like Stick always looked at Amy—only more seriously.

"Cute play, huh?" Cissy asked.

Natalie agreed.

"Don't you think it would be about the greatest thing in the world to be an actress?" the older girl went on.

Natalie tried to hide her surprise. Sure, it would be helpful at times—like now—to be able to act like you weren't scared, or nervous, or dowdy. Out loud, however, she admitted, "I doubt that I have an ounce of acting talent."

"I'd *love* it," Cissy said dreamily, ignoring Natalie's remark.

"We'd better go back in if we don't want to miss anything," Scott suggested.

Ron grabbed Cissy's hand, still gazing at her adoringly. She leaned toward him and whispered something in his ear as they strolled off toward the building.

When Natalie reached the door, Scott was there to hold it open for her.

"Hey, you two," Cissy called back over her shoulder, "why don't you plan to go out for a bite with us after the play?"

Natalie cringed, feeling even younger than her sixteen years. "Thanks, but I have to go straight home."

The beautiful blonde smiled as if it didn't really matter. "Okay. See ya!"

When they returned to their seats, Natalie wondered what would happen if she put her arm on the armrest again. Would Scott hold her hand? Some of the boys from church—just friends—had tried that at movies. But she had always found some way to avoid the issue—like sticking her hand into a bag of popcorn. Still, she realized, giving him a quick glance, she wouldn't mind if Scott held her hand. But he was holding on to his program.

As Act II began, the hilarious dialogue brought more ripples of laughter from the audience, and Natalie was soon caught up in the action. The butler's "body" began appearing in the strangest places—the maid's closet, under her bed, outside her window. At a rapid pace, the mystery unfolded, leaving them all gasping for breath by the end of the play.

The actors deserved the standing ovation the audience gave them, Natalie decided.

"I loved it," Natalie could say honestly when she and Scott headed back toward Garden City. "But I'm sorry I caused you to miss out on being with Cissy and Ron."

"That's okay," Scott replied as he pulled out onto the main road. For an instant Natalie wondered if his passive attitude was due to his watching for traffic, or if he was welcoming the chance to get rid of her early in the evening.

"I was surprised to see Cissy at the play," Natalie

said, hoping to shift the conversation to Scott's family.

"Really?" he asked, glancing her way.

"Well, not surprised that she was at the play, actually. I guess I was just surprised when she said she'd like to be an actress."

"Why is that?"

"Well, Cissy's so elegant that it's just hard to imagine her on stage, running around and yelling like those actresses tonight."

Scott laughed. It was a nice rumbling sound, sort of deep and pleasant. "I guess it is a little hard to believe. Just like those stories you told me about your family. When I met your mother and sisters, they seemed so quiet and polite."

It was Natalie's turn to giggle. "I guess people are not always what they seem."

"You're right about that."

At that moment, lights from an oncoming car swept his face, and Natalie could see the tensed muscle in his jaw. Something was bothering him. Natalie wondered what it was and if his remark had anything to do with it. Or was he talking about Cissy . . . or *her*?

She shook off the disturbing thoughts. Even if Scott didn't have any romantic interest in her, maybe they could still be friends. Besides, she didn't think he would deliberately make an unkind remark. He seemed too polite for that. "I guess I really don't know Cissy very well," she confessed.

Scott shrugged. "She's okay, when you get to know her."

"Oh, I'm sure she is." Natalie hoped she hadn't given the impression that she thought otherwise. "She

. . . um . . . models, doesn't she?"

He nodded. "For Belk's, mostly. Occasionally, she has other shows."

"She could be a professional, she's so beautiful."

Scott smiled. "So is your sister," he said, then groaned and slapped his forehead with the heel of one hand. "I don't mean that you're *not*. It's just . . ."

"Don't worry about it, Scott. It's all right." Natalie meant it. "I've had fourteen years to get used to that. It's just a fact of life."

"I really like the way *you* look, Natalie," he said gallantly, and although her heart leaped a little at that remark, she thought it still sounded like an apology.

"Thanks," she mumbled. "I do, too. It would be way too embarrassing to be stared at the way people stare at Amy and Cissy."

He smiled. "Yeah, it's hard sometimes . . . for Cissy, I mean," he added quickly.

Natalie had the feeling he might have been talking about himself. He had to know what everyone at school said about him—that he was "a good-looking guy with a cranberry red sports car." And that was *all* she knew about him—except that he was the nephew of Martha Brysen, and she didn't want to mention that. It might lead to a discussion she wasn't eager to get into with Scott Lambert.

"Does Cissy live in Garden Acres, too?" Natalie asked a leading question.

He nodded but changed the subject, and his next words surprised her. "I think Cissy could use a friend like you."

"*Me?*" Natalie figured Cissy had all the friends she

needed. She ran around with a wealthy clique at school, she had a part-time modeling job and a college-age boyfriend. *What in the world does she need with a friend like me?* Natalie wondered.

"What I mean is," Scott went on to explain, "right now, Cissy isn't getting along with her folks. You seem to do that okay."

"Well, my parents make the rules."

"Don't you ever feel like breaking them?"

Natalie was thoughtful as she stared down at the program she intended to keep as a souvenir of this night. Then she looked over at Scott, but his eyes seemed glued to the road. Why would he ask a question like that? "Sure I do," she admitted after a moment. "It would be nice if I could have decided whether or not to go eat with Cissy and Ron, for instance. But I have a curfew. And if I'm not home by eleven, I suffer the consequences."

He glanced her way, then back at the road. "But you don't get mad at your folks?"

"Sometimes. But I know they love me and want the best for me, even if I don't always agree."

"Suppose you knew they were wrong about something you really wanted," he asked, probing. "What would you do then?"

Scott was asking some tough questions, and she wasn't sure how to answer him. She and her parents were pretty much on the same wavelength, and they explained their reasons when they disagreed with her. "I don't know the answer," she finally said. "I think I would pray about it first. Then, if God didn't change my parents' minds, I'd try to accept that."

He smiled, still watching the road. "It figures." There was a long silence before he added, "Maybe we could go out with Cissy and Ron sometime."

Is he asking for another date?

Before Natalie could decide just what Scott had meant, he turned off the highway, headed for Garden City, and abruptly changed the subject. "John Kemp said there was a lockdown at the prison last week. Was your dad in on that?"

The rest of the way home she answered more questions about her dad's work. It was ten minutes before eleven o'clock when he pulled up in front of her house. He immediately got out and came around to open her door, but she beat him by a second or two.

"You don't need to walk me to the door," Natalie said quickly. The porch light flooded the lawn with a bright golden glow.

"I don't mind."

Her thoughts raced as they walked to the front door. Would he try to kiss her? If so, would she let him? She should have had a breath mint. But maybe that would have been like asking for it.

When they reached the stoop, he paused, "Thanks, Natalie. I enjoyed tonight."

"Me too," she said, looking up at him, her heart in her throat. "I had a really good time." This was it! The time he might try to kiss her.

"Well, good-night," he said, then turned and walked toward his car.

She heard him drive away as she stepped inside the living room and shut the door behind her. An uneasiness had settled about her, but she didn't know why.

"Hi, honey," her mom said as she walked into the room with a bowl of popcorn and a glass of soda. "How did your date go?"

Natalie helped herself to a handful of popcorn, then proceeded to tell her mother about the play.

Jill watched her intently, listening as Natalie rattled on, then asked the all-important question, "And did you like Scott?"

Natalie sighed and looked toward the ceiling for an instant, then back at her mother. "He was really nice, Mom."

"But?"

Natalie shrugged. "But what?"

"Why are you not as excited about him now as you were before your date?"

Natalie took a deep breath and plunged in. "It's just that I don't know Scott Lambert any better now than I did before I went out with him. He found out a lot about me and our family, but he's still . . . mysterious."

Her mother glanced at her strangely. "Maybe next time."

There wasn't much chance of that, Natalie thought wryly. "Maybe."

Long after she'd turned out her light and gone to bed, Natalie was replaying the events of the evening.

Next time, her mother had said.

Why did Natalie think there might not be a next time? Was it because of what Katlyn had told her—that Scott had dated several girls only once? And what was that vague nagging sensation she'd had about the evening? They had talked, laughed, joked, and generally had a good time. But . . . something was missing.

Suddenly, she faced the truth.

Scott didn't like her. At least he didn't like her . . . in a special kind of way.

Why? Because she wasn't beautiful like Amy and Cissy? Because she didn't run with the "right crowd"? Still, there was that comment about wanting her to be Cissy's friend. And why had Scott questioned her about doing something her parents wouldn't approve of? Was that his way of finding out what kind of girl she was?

He'd also mentioned going out again—sometime.

Natalie was more confused than ever about Scott. Like she had told her mother, Scott Lambert was still very much a mystery.

Or maybe there was no mystery at all. The simple fact was—her date with Scott had not led to an invitation to the prom!

————

Early the next morning, Natalie was awakened by a knock on the door. It was Amy. "Phone, Nat. It's Ruthie."

Natalie sat up and yawned, then reached for the phone.

"Can I listen?" Amy pleaded.

"Sure." Natalie laughed lightly as memories of last night chased away her sleepiness. There wasn't a single thing she minded her younger sister overhearing. No hand holding, no good-night kiss, no prom invitation.

"Sorry," Natalie said to Ruthie. "It was past eleven before I finished talking to Mom. I thought that was kind of late to be calling your house."

"You're forgiven," Ruthie bubbled. "Now tell me everything!"

Although Natalie didn't tell her "everything," Ruthie managed to read between the lines. "You like him, don't you? Well, maybe when he asks you to go steady, we can be a foursome."

"My parents would never let me go steady at my age," Natalie put in quickly, "and besides, Scott is not known for dating girls more than once."

"Did he ask you to the prom?"

"Nope."

Ruthie was disappointed. "It's still early."

"We'll see."

"See you at church," Ruthie said.

When Natalie hung up, Amy had stars in her eyes. "I can hardly wait till I can date."

Natalie playfully pushed Amy out the door so she could get dressed. At that moment, she felt light years older than her fourteen-year-old sister. Amy had no idea that a date could leave you wondering if you were special . . . or a dud. But then, Amy would probably never have that problem.

———

With Sunday morning being the frantic crunch it usually was, the Ainsworths rarely sat down together for breakfast. Natalie was eating cereal at the kitchen table when her dad came in and pulled out a chair.

After a moment's hesitation, he launched the conversation. "Your mother said the date went well."

Natalie nodded. He seemed pleased when she told him that Scott had asked about his work at the prison.

"Before the date, you said you didn't know much about the young man. Did you learn any more?"

"Not really . . . except that he has an older brother."

Her dad's eyes were riveted on the table thoughtfully.

"What do you know about him, Dad?" she asked, feeling that funny kind of dread again.

"It's no secret that his parents aren't together," he said. "I don't know any of the details, but I've heard rumors. Anyway, it isn't Scott's fault," he added quickly. "And since he didn't volunteer the information, it might be best not to mention it to him. Besides," he admonished, "it's not our place to judge people."

Natalie nodded miserably. She had gone on and on about her wonderful, happy family. She had felt that Scott wanted to hear about them, but it must have made him feel awful that his parents were not together—whatever the reason.

During the afternoon, Natalie watched the video and read material about the youth abstinence program. She thought about it for a while, prayed, then came up with a stand she felt would best represent the youth group.

What she still didn't know was whether Scott would ask her to the prom. *Oh well*, she tried to console herself, *there's always Craig or Philip*. At least she wouldn't be without a date. If Scott didn't ask her by

Wednesday, she'd have to decide which boy she wanted to go with.

Not having a date to the prom was nothing short of a disaster. *And I have three possibilities,* she thought confidently as she brushed her wavy brown hair. *I'm really lucky.*

But the blue eyes in the mirror did not twinkle back at her, and the lips weren't turned up in her usual smile.

Five

"If you're not going to the prom with me, Natalie, I'm going to ask Junie Crawford," Philip said later at church. "Her brother told me nobody'd asked her yet."

Great approach! Natalie thought. What else could she say but, "Sure, go ahead."

He turned a little pink. "Thanks. Besides, I know you're dating Scott now."

"One rose does not a summer make, Philip," Natalie corrected him, quoting a phrase her mother often used.

Philip shrugged as if he didn't know what she was talking about. "I don't blame you," he said dejectedly. "I don't even have a car."

Natalie stared after him as he sauntered away, shaking her head. How could things get so confused? What she had learned to like about Scott had nothing to do with his car.

After church, she saw Philip talking to Junie.

"If Scott doesn't ask me by Wednesday," she told Ruthie, "I'm going to tell Craig I'll go with him." She had begun to feel a little jittery about it. The prom was less than ten days away.

"If you had an almost-steady like me," Ruthie goaded her, "you wouldn't have to worry."

Not about a prom date, Natalie was thinking. But she had already explained to Ruthie that her parents felt she was too young for a steady. And there was a practical side, too. Sometimes, if you dated a guy more than once, other guys seemed to think you were off limits. Going steady could be too confining. Andy and Stephanie had talked about it being too tempting as well.

"Well, I like having a special boyfriend," Ruthie had said more than once. "I never have to worry about having someone to go out with."

Most of the time, Natalie didn't agree with her friend on that issue. But lately, the unpleasant thought of going dateless to the prom, or not going at all, churned her stomach into cottage cheese.

"Don't worry," Ruthie soothed. "There's still time for Scott to ask you."

––––––––

"Don't worry," Jill echoed shortly before Natalie left to attend the board meeting at church.

Natalie wasn't nearly as worried about representing the youth group as she was about running into Scott's aunt Martha Brysen.

As it turned out, that was exactly what happened. When Natalie walked in, Mrs. Johnson, the missionary society leader, patted the empty seat next to her. Sitting directly across the conference table was Mrs. Brysen.

"Hello, Natalie," the woman spoke in a pleasant voice. "How are you this afternoon?"

"Just fine, thank you," Natalie said, then sat down next to Mrs. Johnson, who began making small talk.

Natalie answered her questions, but her eyes kept wandering to the woman sitting across from her. Mrs. Brysen seemed to be sneaking glances at her, too. Did she know that Scott had taken her out? Was she the kind of girl Mrs. Brysen would want Scott to date?

Mrs. Brysen bore a marked resemblance to Cissy, and it seemed strange to think of Cissy's aunt as a once-beautiful young woman. Nor had Natalie noticed before that Mrs. Brysen's wavy gray hair fell softly to one side of her face, and was pushed back on the other—a style similar to Cissy's. The older woman looked chic in her dove gray suit and soft silk blouse.

Natalie wore the Easter suit she'd worn Saturday night with Scott, but with a pink blouse today. It was the dressiest outfit she owned, and she had wanted to appear as mature as possible for the meeting.

Soon, other board members filtered in and filled the empty spaces around the table. Pastor Darlee took a seat at the head and called the meeting to order with a brief prayer.

Natalie lifted her head and looked at the pastor, as did the others. "Our only item of business this afternoon is the youth abstinence program," he began.

Thump! Thump! Thump! There went my heart, Natalie thought. This was worse than sitting by Scott for almost two hours during the play. How in the world could she talk about sex in front of all these adults? Maybe she should just slip under the table and hide! Instead, she breathed her own silent prayer. *Please help me, Lord.*

As if in answer to that prayer, a thought jumped into her head. When the youth group had voted her in as president, she had just turned sixteen. She'd expressed her doubts to Stephanie, pointing out that there were older, more experienced members.

"But the group voted for *you*," Stephanie reminded her. "And one thing you need to remember—when you lead, don't be self-conscious. Try to concentrate on what Jesus would want you to do."

No better time to start than now, Natalie decided.

When Pastor Darlee asked if everyone in the room had reviewed the materials, there were nods of affirmation. Then his eyes met Natalie's, and he asked the question she had been dreading. "Since you're representing the youth group, Natalie, we'd like to hear from them."

Natalie cleared her throat and clasped her fingers together on her lap so no one would see them trembling. "Well . . . the youth group voted *for* the program."

"But they don't really know what it's about, do they?" the pastor probed gently.

"No," Natalie admitted. "And I think that's an important point. They voted for it because they know Andy and Stephanie believe it would be good for us. If the program is not voted in, I think it's going to hurt our leaders' feelings and make them feel they're not really in charge."

After a long silence, as if everyone was thinking, one of the older men spoke up. Jim Parill was often referred to as a "pillar" of the church. The white-haired man had been a leader as far back as Natalie could remember. One of his grandsons was in Rose's room at school.

"I can see this young woman's point," Mr. Parill said, addressing the pastor instead of Natalie. "But we can't let Andy's and Stephanie's personal feelings enter into such a far-reaching decision. After all," he said, with a touch of humor in his voice, "even the pastor has to get the board's approval on some of his programs."

Natalie hadn't known that. She glanced at Pastor Darlee, who was joining in with the low chuckles that rumbled around the table, but she thought he looked uncomfortable. He was clicking his ball-point pen in and out. She'd caught herself doing that sometimes at youth meetings when she was uncertain about how to respond to certain questions.

He put down the pen. "I'd like to hear the opinion of everyone on this committee. Let's start with you, Jim," he encouraged kindly, looking the man directly in the eye. "What do you think about this program?"

"No offense to our youth leaders or this young lady here," he said, sending Natalie a quick glance and a smile, "but I tend to go along with what Martha said at the last meeting. She expressed my sentiments exactly—only more eloquently than I ever could."

Mrs. Brysen acknowledged his comment with a pleased expression and a slight nod, and Natalie's heart sank.

Several others spoke up, and Natalie was surprised to find that the group seemed about equally divided on the matter. Then it was Mrs. Brysen's turn. For some reason, she zeroed in on Natalie, addressing her remarks to her. Natalie hoped it was only because they were seated across the table from each other.

"Of course, I advocate abstinence," Scott's aunt asserted. "But I believe that if we implement a new program, it should be to train *parents* on how to educate their children at home."

A couple of other adults agreed that Mrs. Brysen had made a good point. Perhaps the parents *had* failed. Perhaps they should be the ones to instruct their teens instead of leaving it up to the youth leaders.

The missionary leader had another slant on the matter. "I think Martha's right in making the point about parental responsibility," she said. "However, the subject of sex is no longer private. The numbers of teen pregnancies and disease have made it public."

"It seems to me," Mrs. Brysen rebutted, "that when you prohibit something, it only becomes that much more popular. And, too, when one becomes a Christian, he or she is vowing to live by the values taught by Jesus Christ. This program calls for an *additional* vow. That seems redundant to me."

As Mrs. Brysen spoke, Natalie began to understand her dad's and Andy's attitude toward her—and maybe even Jim Parill's. Cissy's aunt stated her point of view in such an intelligent but charming way. She was not at all overbearing about it, as Natalie had assumed she would be. It was obvious that she really had the youth group's best interests at heart. And there was no question that her opinions were based on Christian principles.

In fact, Natalie found herself agreeing with Mrs. Brysen's arguments. The church *should* teach parents how to talk to their children about sex. The Bible *was* very explicit about the body being the temple of God. And when people became Christians, they *did* vow to follow the teachings of Jesus—including those on sexual purity.

"This program," Mrs. Brysen went on, "brings sex into the church. It has already invaded every other area of our lives, particularly through television and advertising. Some things should be kept strictly private and personal—and this is one of them."

Silence permeated the room for a moment as her comments registered. Finally, Pastor Darlee turned again to Natalie. "We know how Andy and Stephanie feel about the program and how the youth group voted, but I'm sure we would all like to know *your* opinion."

She drew a deep breath and plunged in. "Well, I think it's true that we should listen to our parents and read our Bibles—and most of us in the youth group do know right from wrong. . . ." She waited for a moment, gathering her thoughts. Then, making eye contact with Mrs. Brysen, she said bravely, "But I didn't know all the statistics until I watched the video and read the materials. The Bible tells us to be ready to give reasons for what we believe. The video and written material state those reasons."

"Then you are in favor of the program?" the pastor asked.

Now Natalie didn't dare look at Mrs. Brysen and the others who had sided with her. What if her next words blew her chance with Scott? "Yes, for many reasons." She tried to remember the notes she had jotted down as she studied the materials. "Some of the members of the youth group don't come from strong Christian families like mine. And although most parents encourage their children to tell them everything, a lot of teens I know *don't*."

"But this public stand"—Mrs. Brysen began, looking at the board members—"I'm just not sure it's right. After all, Christians are to set an example, not flaunt their morality."

"Jesus said to reveal our belief in Him by the way we live our lives. I think that includes making some public stands," the missionary leader reminded her.

"Also," Natalie added, "a lot of people don't have strong beliefs, or don't know how to express them. They're afraid of being 'different.' This program gives them the chance to be part of a crowd—a crowd that stands for the right things."

Six

By Wednesday Natalie had not heard how the church leaders voted, nor had Scott asked her to the prom. She had not seen him at school, either, and wondered if he had been skipping study hall just to avoid running into her. But that was silly. Scott seemed like the kind of person who would still be polite and friendly, even if he didn't like a girl enough to want to date her again.

Natalie even entertained the idea that Cissy might come strolling down the hall and fill her in on Scott's whereabouts. But it didn't happen.

What did happen was that Katlyn Chander made a point after study hall of standing in the hallway, where Natalie would be sure to see her. She flipped her black hair behind her shoulders. "How's it going, Nat?" she purred.

"Everything's super," Natalie replied, knowing that wasn't what Katlyn wanted to hear, and moved on down the hall.

Katlyn caught up with her. "I mean . . . how was the date?"

"Which one?" Natalie asked innocently.

"You know"—Katlyn persisted, her honeyed tone growing thick with exasperation—"with *Scott*."

"Oh, that," Natalie replied nonchalantly. "Nice. I had a good time."

"What did you do?"

Natalie shot her a quick glance.

"Oh, I don't mean *that*!" Katlyn gave a dismissive wave of her hand. "Everyone knows you're a goody-two-shoes."

"I am not!" Natalie denied, bristling. "I'm a Christian."

"Well, who isn't?" Katlyn said defensively. "I'm not exactly a heathen, but nobody's ever called me a goody-two-shoes."

"Nobody ever called me that, either," Natalie returned, "except you."

"You mean, not to your face," Katlyn said smugly.

Natalie felt herself grow hot with anger. She reminded herself what the Bible said about a gentle answer turning away anger. But at the moment, she couldn't think of a gentle answer. Anyway, she couldn't imagine that Katlyn's crowd stood around discussing Natalie Ainsworth! Obviously, Ruthie was right—Katlyn was just plain jealous.

"Look," Natalie began, supplying just enough information to get Katlyn off her back, "Scott took me to see a play. We had a good time. And that's it."

"I warned you, didn't I?"

"Warned me?"

"That Scott would never ask you out again. I guess I'm the only girl in school he's ever dated more than once."

Natalie tried to hide her surprise, but from the pleased look on Katlyn's face, she knew she hadn't been successful. Had Scott dated her to make Katlyn jealous? Cruel as it was, that sort of thing happened sometimes.

"Yeah," Katlyn said confidently. "We live in the same neighborhood, you know." She waited for that to register with Natalie.

So, Katlyn lived in Garden Acres, too. Well, that wasn't surprising, Natalie thought. She was one of the more popular drama-club juniors who ran around with some of the seniors. When Natalie didn't respond, Katlyn continued, "Scott and I go to the same church, so I see him a lot. He and I double-dated with Cissy and Ron, you know."

No, Natalie *didn't* know. She didn't want to feel hurt, but it hurt anyway. As a leader in her church and school groups, Natalie had always been the one to warn others about falling into the dangerous trap of trying to get even. But now that she was being put to the test, it wasn't easy to practice what she preached. She bit back the sharp reply on the end of her tongue.

So what if Scott Lambert never asked her for another date? So what if Scott had dated Katlyn several times? That didn't mean he'd made a lifetime commitment, did it? But all the explanations in the world didn't make the sick feeling go away.

———

"Zowie!" Amy exclaimed at the supper table. "I think I should hang a sign around my neck saying, 'I'm only fourteen and I can't date!'" She flung out her

81

hands in exasperation. "Would you believe that two seniors have asked me to the prom—besides a ton of juniors?" She glanced at her father. "Not all of them were jerks, either, Dad. So anytime you're ready to let me date, I'd like to be the first to know."

He frowned over his glasses. "Don't even consider it for a couple of years, young lady."

"And don't refer to boys as 'jerks,' Amy," her mother reprimanded, refilling her iced tea glass. "That's worse than 'hunks.' "

"Sure is!" Amy agreed, to the utter delight of her youngest sister, who giggled behind her hand. "What did you call boys that were . . . um"—Amy searched for a word—"not cool?"

"Well," her mother began reluctantly, "I'll admit we did have a name for them." Amy and her sisters were all ears. "Nerds," she finished weakly.

"And what did you call the girls who didn't measure up?" Natalie asked their dad.

He glanced up, cast a doubtful look at his wife, and took a chance. "Airheads."

"Oh," Jill put in above the laughter that followed his announcement, "maybe that's what was meant when we talked about some of those pesky boys who kept hanging around. We'd say, 'I wouldn't give him air if he were in a jug.' "

"Frankly," said Sarah with a bored expression on her face, "I'm never going to date."

"Why?" All heads swiveled toward the twelve-year-old.

"Why do you say that, honey?" her mother asked, looking worried.

"It makes people crazy. I mean, Marcie went to a movie with Tim. Now, she brings makeup to school— she's not allowed to wear it—and paints her face. Then she stands around and giggles with the other girls who've had dates." Sarah looked hurt. "She's . . . different. No fun to be with anymore. She used to be my friend, but now she won't even play basketball."

Amy changed the subject. "Has Scott asked you to the prom yet, Nat?"

"I haven't seen him. We have study hall together, but he hasn't been there all week. Anyway, I don't expect him to ask me." Uncomfortable with the sympathetic look her sister was giving her, she quickly added, "Both Philip and Craig asked me, but I told Philip to go ahead and invite Junie Crawford. Tonight at church, I'll tell Craig I'll go with him. He's . . . not so bad."

"But he's not as cute as Scott," Amy said.

Natalie shrugged, trying to ignore the tight little knot in the pit of her stomach. "I had a life before Scott. I'll have one after. Oh, I forgot to tell you, Amy. Stephanie called and said the youth abstinence program has been approved. Gotta run. Have to shower and get ready."

"So do I," Amy suddenly remembered. "We'd better hurry!"

———

"There's Craig!" Amy said excitedly as soon as Natalie drove into the church parking lot. He was getting out of his dad's car with several of his friends, including Philip and Stick. "Why don't you tell him now?"

"Craig," Natalie called, hanging back a little after

the others sprinted on toward the door of the church. "About the prom—"

Before she could finish, he lifted his hand. "Not to worry, Nat. I didn't think you'd go with me anyway. So me and Philip are double-dating. I asked Stacey. She's a friend of Junie's, you know." He put his thumb and forefinger together. "It's A-okay."

"Thanks," she mumbled as he moved to catch up with the guys.

Amy looked devastated. "What are you going to do, Natalie? You just *have* to go to the prom. And you've *got* to have a date."

"I don't . . . and I don't," Natalie retorted and was immediately sorry. She remembered mentioning to Ruthie last week that she'd rather go alone than with one of the boys from church she'd known all her life. But that was before Cissy had told her Scott might invite her.

A vague uneasiness made her stomach ache. Could Scott and Cissy have been playing some kind of joke on her? Cissy had never paid her any attention before. And Scott didn't even know her. She wasn't in their league socially, that was for sure. But that part didn't bother Natalie. She was satisfied—happy, really—with her family situation, even though she knew that not everyone felt the way she did. Some people valued others on the basis of how much money they had or where they lived. Were Cissy and Scott like that? And how did Katlyn fit into the picture?

Natalie sure didn't know the answers to those questions. But she was determined to forget Scott Lambert and return to being the happy, carefree girl she used to be.

———

At the meeting, Andy and Stephanie were on cloud nine. "The church leaders approved the program," Andy was saying just as he was interrupted by the sound of a basketball being dribbled in the hallway.

In popped Stick with Brad right behind him. "Sorry!" Stick said when he realized he was late.

"I hope you showered," Ruthie badgered him as he pulled out a chair and placed it behind her.

"What do you call this?" he asked, touching his finger to his forehead and demonstrating the wetness by wiping it on her arm.

"Sweat!"

"But it's clean sweat!" He glanced toward Amy, who was sitting with her friends, but she turned her head away.

The guys laughed and the girls groaned as Stick slumped into his chair. "Excuuuse me. Go right ahead," he said, giving Andy a mock salute.

Andy shook his head in dismay. "Thank you very much, Stick. As I was saying, the church leaders have approved the abstinence program but added some stipulations."

"Now we like the program even better," Stephanie put in before anyone could object.

Andy nodded. "We're going to focus on *all* areas of our lives, not just the sexual. How do you feel about having a ceremony in church in front of the whole congregation? That way the members can understand what we're doing and why."

Several groaned. Some said it was a great idea. Others weren't sure. "Can't we just do it here?"

"We need to emphasize to others and to ourselves how important this commitment is. It's like taking a vow when you get married," Stephanie explained. "We don't just 'jump the broom.' "

"Jump the broom?" Eyebrows went up at the idea.

"Oh, my great-great-great-grandmama and grandpapa did that," said Twila Jones, who lifted her pretty brown face and tilted her head a little to the side when she was about to say something significant. "The slaves used to do that when they fell in love. In some places, they weren't allowed to get married in a church like white folks, so they put a broom down at the threshold of their little cabin, made their own vow before God, and jumped over that broom. That did it! They were married. Oooh," she moaned and clapped her hand over her mouth, looking at Stephanie. "I ruined your point, didn't I?"

Stephanie laughed and shook her head. "Not really. It gives me a chance to explain about making a vow. The vows we make to God are more important than the promises we make to people. In your ancestors' case, Twila, they had no choice but to do what the slave master allowed. It was their way of making a promise to each other. But for those of us who do have the opportunity, we need to take Jesus' word seriously and let our light shine for Him. We're to live our lives according to what we believe all the time."

Lana was still skeptical. "What if some people don't want to take a vow?"

"That's okay," Stephanie assured her. "Just like some of the church leaders weren't sure about this program, it's okay if some of you are not comfortable with it. You'll still be a part of our group, and there will be other things you can do to honor God."

"What about the stipulations?" Ruthie asked.

"That's the good part," Andy said. "We've decided not to concentrate only on sexual abstinence but to cover purity in general. We'll renew our vows periodically in all aspects of our spiritual life."

He gestured toward the plastic bag near Stephanie, who began setting the small white boxes on the table. "Now, to start things off, Steph and I are going to have our own little ceremony."

Stephanie stood behind the table. "Andy and I wouldn't ask you to do something we're not willing to do first. So this is our pledge to you. We will try our best to keep our minds and bodies pure and to be an example for you."

"And these are our gifts to you," Andy said, coming to stand beside her. "They're symbols of our purity, and we hope they will become yours, too. Stand, please."

The group shuffled to their feet. They had never been so quiet, Natalie thought. Everyone was waiting to see what would happen next.

Andy opened his Bible and flipped a few pages, running his finger down the page to find a verse before looking up. "Jesus gave us a super promise in the Sermon on the Mount when He said, 'Blessed are the pure in heart, *for they will see God.*'"

Stephanie followed, her Bible open to 2 Corinthians. "And as if that weren't enough, Paul goes on to give us some more promises and to tell us how we can receive them: 'For we are the temple of the living God.

As God has said: "I will live with them and walk among them, and I will be their God, and they will be my people.

" 'Therefore, come out from them and be separate,' says the Lord. 'Touch no unclean thing, and I will receive you. . . .'

" 'Since we have these promises, dear friends, let us purify ourselves from *everything* that contaminates *body* and *spirit*, perfecting holiness out of reverence for God.' "

There was a hush in the room as the words registered. Then the spell was broken as Andy and Stephanie began to hand out the small boxes.

Everyone took their places and began to untie the little white ribbons. Natalie and Ruthie made a game of undoing one side of the paper, slipping out the little box, lifting the lid, and then the square of cotton.

"Oh, how sweet," Ruthie breathed.

Natalie picked up the tiny white dove and held it in the palm of her hand. Sculpted in profile, the little bird's wings were spread in flight, with a gold dot indicating one eye. "Beautiful," she murmured.

She looked over at Stephanie, who was leaning back against the table. Natalie went up and hugged her. Ruthie was next, with all the other girls close behind.

"Thanks . . . I think," mumbled some of the guys to Andy.

"Getting jewelry is not the worst thing that could happen to a guy," Andy said good-naturedly, having anticipated their reaction.

"You can carry these little doves in your change purse—" Stephanie began.

"What if we don't have a change purse?" quipped Stick.

"I was getting to that. Or . . . you guys can carry them in your pants pockets and, when you pull out your change, you'll be reminded of your promise."

By that time, Stick was standing with his pockets hanging out. No change!

Stephanie ignored the snickers. "My uncle's a jeweler, so if some of you girls want to turn your dove into a pin, or wear it on a chain or bracelet, he can take care of that. The guys might want to make theirs into a tie tack or lapel pin."

"When do we get the suit?" Stick asked. That brought a few laughs and "Yeahs," which relieved the slight tension among the boys.

"Well, the point is to put it somewhere so you can see it to remind you of God's Spirit," Andy said. "It's not something you're obligated to wear."

———

"I really like what the church leaders added to the program," Ruthie said when Natalie was driving her home after the meeting. "Loving while we're waiting."

Amy opened her box. "A little white dove . . ."

Natalie smiled. " . . . symbolizing pure love."

———

"Fourteen-carat gold?" Jill said, squinting to read the fine print etched on the back of the dove when Natalie and Amy got home. "This is really nice. And it looks expensive."

"Let me see," Rose said, coming over from the

couch where she was watching TV in her robe.

While Rose examined Amy's charm, Natalie told her mother the ideas Stephanie had for the doves. "I'd like to have mine made into a pin."

"I'll see if Jim can take it to the jeweler in the morning."

"How could they afford it, Mom?" Natalie asked, concerned. "I don't think Andy and Stephanie have much money."

"Pretty," Rose said, handing the dove back to Amy. The two girls settled on the couch and dug into the popcorn bowl.

Natalie and Jill followed. "Well, honey, I'm sure Stephanie and Andy know what they're doing. Sometimes people sacrifice for something they really want— like we do for vacations. You know how your dad and I do without things when we're saving for something special."

Natalie pondered for a moment. "But Andy and Stephanie talk about having just enough to live on after paying their tithe and the bills. And look at us, Mom." She lifted a handful of popcorn. "Here we are, pigging out, while they might be going hungry."

"Oh, Natalie, they're grown people. They're not going to starve," Sarah put in, coming into the room and overhearing the last of the conversation. She helped herself to some popcorn. "They could call up someone at the church and invite themselves to dinner."

"But they wouldn't."

Jill sighed. "If you're worried, honey, then do something about it."

"Like what?"

"Give them a pounding."

Hand poised over the popcorn bowl, Rose looked puzzled. "You mean, beat them up so they won't notice how hungry they are?"

Jill and the girls laughed.

"A pounding, my little buggy-boo," Jill said, reaching over to tickle her youngest child, "is when you ask people to donate food to give to someone who needs it."

"Like people do at Christmas?" Rose asked.

Natalie and her mother exchanged glances, then Jill expressed what they were both thinking. "We should be helping people in need all year long, not just on special occasions."

"I can call the telephone committee and get things started," Natalie said, suddenly inspired.

"I can pick up some boxes from the grocery store after I drop Rose off at school in the morning," Jill said.

"And I'll decorate the boxes," offered Rose, obviously still thinking about Christmas.

———

By the time the girls got home from school the next afternoon, boxes were piled in the playroom. Rose was painting watercolor landscapes on a roll of freezer paper their dad had brought from the corner grocer's.

"I like impressionism," she explained when Natalie looked over her shoulder.

"Where did you learn to do that?"

"In art, at school."

"You're really interested in art, aren't you?"

Rose looked up shyly and, deciding that Natalie was not making fun of her, nodded and grinned.

"I couldn't do anything like that if my life depended on it," Natalie said, rather in awe of her little sister.

"Aw, you're good at *everything*."

Natalie touched her shoulder affectionately. That was nice to hear, but she couldn't think of a single thing she excelled in—except, maybe, her schoolwork. Amy, of course, was talented in cheering, which took a lot of athletic ability and coordination.

When Sarah appeared at the doorway, carrying her new gerbil cage, Natalie was aware that this sister hadn't shown any particular talent, either.

"Gerald is lonely. I'm going out to let him see Pongo."

"Okay," Rose said indifferently, thoroughly engrossed in what she was doing.

"You're not going to take him out of the cage, are you?" Natalie asked.

"Of course not!"

Natalie thought Sarah seemed insulted and looked a little sad, even though she'd gotten the pet she'd asked for. Maybe she just wanted attention.

———

Early Saturday morning, Rose was up early, knocking on Natalie's door. She waited timidly before being invited in. "You awake?"

Natalie rolled over. "I am now."

"Better get up."

Natalie knew it was useless to try going back to

sleep. Besides, they did have a big day ahead. "You've done so much to help with the boxes, Rose, and Sarah hasn't done anything. Let's get her to fill them."

After pulling on some old cutoffs and a tank top, Natalie went downstairs with Rose and walked into Sarah's room. "Get up, sleepyhead. We need your help."

Sarah covered her head, her words muffled beneath the spread. "You don't need me."

"Yes we do. We need you to help fill the boxes. Come on. The guys will be here anytime now."

"Then let *them* do it."

"You can go with us, if you want to," Natalie suggested. "You'll be in the youth group in less than a year, you know."

"I'll wait," she said and covered her head again.

Giving up, Natalie and Rose shrugged their shoulders and left the room.

Before long, the gang arrived, just in time to begin receiving items from several church members who dropped by. With the extra help, the boxes were filled in record time.

"Where's Stick?" Ruthie asked, noticing that the lanky athlete was missing.

Nobody knew.

Finally Brad asked, "Do you have a basketball hoop?"

"Out back."

The two went to look while the others loaded the cars. Sure enough, Stick was giving Sarah some pointers.

"Your little sis is pretty good," Stick said with a grin.

Sarah turned away and dribbled the ball, but not before Natalie saw the pleased expression on her face. "Yeah," she said as Sarah sent the ball swishing through the net, "she really is, isn't she?"

"Thanks, Stick," Natalie said after they left Sarah to her practice. "That compliment meant a lot to my sister."

"Hey, keep up the good work, pal!" he called to Sarah as he followed Natalie back into the house. "She could make a good player. I mean it."

Natalie could only shake her head. How had they missed it? Sarah had always loved shooting hoops. "What do you know? My sister, the ace!"

"I don't believe this!" Stephanie squealed when two carloads of young people landed on her doorstep around ten o'clock and began hauling in six boxes of groceries. "Andy, come quick!"

Andy looked on in amazement and scratched his head. "Hey, guys, you didn't need to do this."

"Okay, fellas, get the boxes back in the cars," Stick said and reached for one of them.

"Don't you dare!" Stephanie ordered. "I'm so sick of tuna sandwiches I could barf. Andy can have the tuna, and I'll take these boxes."

"You guys are something else." Andy sniffed. At the moment, he looked suspiciously like he had a head cold—or something.

"We've had good training," Ruthie said with a grin.

"Yeah, just call us the White Dove Brigade!" Stick reached into his pocket and took out the little dove.

Stephanie held the screen door open, and the boys stepped forward to help lug the boxes inside. "What made you think of doing a thing like this?" she wanted to know, removing cans from a box and stacking them on the kitchen table.

Natalie answered for the group. "Well, for one thing, we know those doves must have cost you a fortune."

"Uh-oh." Stephanie let out a long breath, still holding a can of soup. "I've mentioned my uncle who's a jeweler?"

They nodded.

"He got the doves for us at cost. And he's letting us make payments when we can."

"Well, it wouldn't have mattered if the doves were free," Natalie said quickly. "We wanted to show our appreciation for all the stuff you do for us."

"Nope!" Stick kidded, reaching for a box. "I think we should take this food to my house!"

This time it was Andy's turn to say, "No way, buddy! All this has whetted my appetite."

———

"Mom, is it okay if I go to Belk's fashion show at the mall tonight?" Natalie asked after she returned from Andy and Stephanie's house. "They're showing prom dresses."

"I want to go, too!" exclaimed Amy.

"Who with?" their mom asked.

"Ruthie. Sean had to visit his aunt this weekend."

Jill made a face. "I'm not too keen on you girls being out late on a Saturday night."

Natalie shrugged. "We could probably get some of the guys to go along."

"I'd feel better about it if you did."

"Stick's always available," Natalie said.

This time Amy's only comment was, "Well, I'm sitting up front with you."

———

When the three girls, Stick, and Brad arrived at Belk's, most of the folding chairs were already taken. "There're three a couple of rows from the back. Take those," Brad said, pointing them out. "Me and Stick can stand in the back."

"Hey," Stick said, noticing a sign that read: SALE—SPRING APPAREL. He put his hand to his forehead and forced his voice an octave higher than usual. "I've just got to get me a new dress to go with my jewelry!"

"I don't know the guy," Amy denied, heading for the chairs with Natalie and Ruthie right behind her. "Never saw him before in my life."

As soon as Natalie settled into her seat, Cissy's boyfriend and Scott, camera on a strap slung over his shoulder, rounded the corner of the portable dressing room. Scott's dark good looks were set off by an open-collared blue shirt. Her heart skipped several beats. *This is what I really came for*, she admitted to herself, feeling she could do with a good scolding. She'd never chased a boy before. Well, she wasn't chasing Scott now. She had just . . . hoped he'd be here.

A couple of older boys about Ron's age began handing out programs. Then a gorgeous woman, her jet black hair slicked back into a French twist at the back of her head, stepped forward and walked down the ramp to the microphone.

Ruthie squirmed. "She makes me feel like a carrot."

"Now quit that!" Natalie smacked her friend's hand playfully. "You're pretty."

"If you like carrots!"

They joined in the applause as the show began. Natalie saw Scott kneel at the front of the ramp, along with some others, adjust his camera, then begin to snap pictures.

The clothes and models were really beautiful—made for each other, she thought. There was constant applause as the girls and guys paraded past in leisure wear, college and career outfits, and evening apparel. For the finale, Cissy stepped out wearing a wedding gown. A chorus of oohs and ahs went up from the audience.

Amy sighed. "She looks just like a bride."

Ruthie nudged Natalie. "I think somebody else thinks so, too."

Natalie followed her glance. Cissy's boyfriend was staring at her as if she was the world's ninth wonder. But no matter how hard she tried to look straight ahead, Natalie's gaze kept swinging toward Scott.

After all the models had pivoted for the last time and were leaving the ramp, the audience rose in a standing ovation, clapping wildly.

At that moment, Scott turned his head in Natalie's direction. Just as he did, a couple of girls came out of the dressing room. One of them was Katlyn Chander.

What was she doing back there? Natalie wondered and decided that she must have been helping the models change.

Seeing the direction of Scott's gaze, Katlyn grabbed his arm and pointed toward something on the other side of the mall. Natalie swallowed a knot of disappointment.

"Act like it doesn't matter," Ruthie advised under her breath.

"Well, it really doesn't," Natalie said with a shrug. But she didn't sound very convincing.

Seven

During the next few days, Natalie thought often of something she'd heard her dad say: "When I was down, a friend told me to cheer up—things could get worse. So I cheered up, and sure enough—things got worse!"

Whoever wrote that line must have been reading my diary! Natalie fumed.

First, her eyes flew right to Scott the moment she entered history class. She hadn't planned to look his way, not wanting him to think he mattered that much to her, one way or the other. Later, however, when she was about to enter study hall, she heard someone say, "Hi, Natalie." Surprised, she turned abruptly and almost ran into him.

"Oh, hi," she said, feeling a sudden rush of heat in her face. *Boy, Ruthie should see me now! Carrot orange can't begin to compare with beet red!*

Scott smiled at her, but his expression looked a little strained, or as her mother would say, "pinched." Something was wrong. Perhaps he thought her feelings were hurt, so to assure him they weren't, she smiled back and said the first thing that popped into her mind.

99

"That was a neat fashion show Saturday night. Cissy looked great."

He nodded, and Natalie thought he was about to say something else when she heard her name called again.

It was Stick!

For one of the few times in her life, she was glad to see him. Anything was better than this awkward encounter with Scott. She smiled encouragingly at Stick and waited for him. Scott got the message and walked on by.

Stick rushed up to her, his tennis shoes scudding on the tile floor. To avoid a collision, he jumped back. "I know you're going to say no, but I talked to Amy," he said, his words tripping over each other like his big feet.

So he talked to Amy, she thought. *Yep, that would be enough to make him stumble all over himself.*

"She said you don't have a date for the prom and that it was okay for me to ask you. She can't go, you know. I guess she just can't stand me." His countenance drooped.

"It's not that, Stick," she said compassionately. "My parents have a rule that we can't date until we're at least sixteen, or whenever we're 'sensible' enough—whichever comes first—and then only under certain conditions. They're strict, that's all."

"Yeah, I know," he said mournfully. "But Amy said it was okay for me to ask you to go with me since you don't have a date."

Feeling rotten about the whole thing and angry with herself for caring and not wanting to go to the prom alone, knowing everyone else already had a date, she figured, *Why not? Scott hasn't asked me.*

In this moment of deliberation, Stick jumped in. "We can ride with Sean and Ruthie. I've already asked him."

At least she'd be with her best friend, Natalie thought. Ruthie made everything fun. It was probably for the best, anyway—being with her friends from church. She should have known better than to date anyone outside that old tried-and-true circle. *Well, live and learn, I always say!*

In fact, it should be a riot, getting Ruthie and Stick together. Each of them could be the life of any gathering—but together, wow! And she wouldn't be sitting on the sidelines when Katlyn Chander made her grand entrance with Scott!

Still, Natalie swallowed a bitter pill of regret when she looked up at Stick and forced a smile. "Sure, I'll go. Thanks for asking me."

"Whew!" he whistled with relief. "Thanks! I thought I'd have to go alone, drown myself in punch, and hope someone had spiked it!"

"None of that," Natalie warned.

The tall boy's face grew serious. "Just kidding, Nat. Come on, you know I'd never touch the stuff."

Before she could apologize for preaching, Stick had turned and ambled down the hallway. She realized she didn't know much about him, just as she didn't know much about Scott. Were all boys so mysterious? When she spotted Stick goofing off with a group of guys farther down the hall, she guessed she hadn't hurt his feelings after all.

Inside the library, and against her better judgment, Natalie sought Scott out. There he was—in one of the study carousels. Catching her eye, he smiled and nodded, and Natalie felt her gaze lock with his. She couldn't help smiling back, feeling that unwanted flutter in her stomach.

What if Scott asked her to the prom after study hall? Would she do the right thing and keep her promise to Stick? A week ago she would have had no question about it. But now, well . . . the decision wasn't as easy to make when emotions were involved, she realized. She breathed a quick prayer, asking God to help her keep her commitment. Rejection was not a very good feeling. She ought to know.

After study hall Natalie took her time gathering her books, then moved slowly out into the hallway, in case Scott wanted to catch up with her. He didn't. But Katlyn was heading her way with a determined look on her face. When they passed in the hall, Natalie returned Katlyn's cool "Hi" but didn't miss the smug look on her face. Oh well, it wasn't Katlyn's fault that she liked Scott—or vice versa. Sometimes you just couldn't help having special feelings for someone— even when you knew better.

———

Since Ruthie had declared that her brother Justin was going to give her a nervous breakdown before she could ever get ready for the prom, it was decided that she would dress at Natalie's house. And when the two girls were finally ready and came down the steps from Natalie's room, they were greeted by applause from the family waiting below.

"Who are these beautiful young women?" Jill asked as Natalie and Ruthie appeared in all their pre-prom splendor.

"A carrot with green leaves," Ruthie replied self-consciously.

"Let me be the judge of that," Jill ordered. "Now turn around and let me see you."

Ruthie pivoted, while Natalie looked on, thinking how lovely her friend looked. The leaf green dress was made along simple lines. Narrow shoulder straps widened at the bodice that met in a V and was adorned with a single row of covered buttons, running from the midriff to just above one knee. Where the material parted, Ruthie playfully exposed a shapely leg. Green pumps to match the dress and a chunky gold bracelet and earrings completed the picture.

"You're absolutely stunning," Jill said.

Amy grinned. "She cleans up real good, doesn't she?"

Little Rose was all eyes. "You're . . . pretty."

Even Sarah said, "I like it."

"Well, I'm too short and dumpy to wear anything like *that*," Ruthie observed, shifting the attention from herself to Natalie.

"You look fab!" Amy gushed when Ruthie moved aside and Natalie stepped into view.

Natalie knew she would have chosen a more "grown-up" dress—perhaps strapless and a little more form-fitting—if she had been going with Scott. But this dress—one she had worn before—was fine for a date with Stick. The black satin material of the bodice lay softly against her skin, with puffed sleeves starting just below the shoulders. She wore the tiny spaghetti straps up, knowing she would feel more comfortable that way.

The bodice tapered into a full black-and-white-checked pouffed skirt that fell to just above her knees. With the dress she wore sheer black hose with black high heels, studded with rhinestone clips. Natalie had let Amy play with her hair again, and now it was pulled back from her face, revealing small rhinestone earrings she had borrowed from her mom.

Just as she was feeling rather pretty, Ruthie dropped a bomb. "D'ya suppose Stick will wear a suit?"

Natalie gasped. She hadn't thought of that. "Maybe he doesn't even have one!"

"Now don't you embarrass that poor boy, Natalie," her mother warned.

"Oh, don't worry, Mrs. A.," Ruthie piped up cheerfully. "He does that all by himself!"

The laughter that followed eased the tension, and Natalie felt more relaxed when they heard Sean's old car rattling down the street.

Amy rushed over to the window. "I'll let you know how Stick's dressed, Nat, so you won't faint when he comes in." She pushed the drape aside and peered out. "Oh no! You won't believe it! *I* don't believe it!"

"What? What?" Everyone except Natalie crowded around the window.

"Wow! Sean looks great!" Ruthie was clearly impressed with her date's blond good looks in his black tuxedo.

"Yeah, but who's that toothpick beside him?" Amy jested.

"Amyyyyy," Jill cautioned.

"Oh, I'm just trying to worry Natalie, Mom."

"I'm worried enough, thank you." Natalie grimaced, hoping she could hide her disappointment in not being with Scott.

When the boys arrived, Ruthie and Sean exchanged compliments, and Natalie was amused to find her friend ducking her head self-consciously. Maybe it was just the unfamiliarity of wearing such fancy clothes.

Natalie thought Stick looked fine in his tux, although his pants were slightly high-water, but it wasn't his fault he was so tall. *At least he isn't wearing his white athletic socks!*

"You look nice, Stick," Natalie said honestly, ignoring the big ears and paintbrush hairdo.

"You do, too," he said, but his gaze was for Amy, who was trying to hide behind the curtain.

"For *us*?" Ruthie quipped as the guys handed them the customary corsage boxes.

Jill pinned the flowers on—yellow roses for Ruthie and white carnations for Natalie. "Perfect!" she exclaimed, stepping back to admire the effect.

The boys drew a sigh of relief.

"You might like to know," Stick said, reaching into his pocket and pulling out a tiny charm, "that I'm carrying my white dove." His shy glance at Amy seemed to say he was carrying it as a commitment to her.

No one recognized the school gym when they arrived for the prom. Round tables, covered with white cloths, dotted the room, and artificial trees flanked a platform where a band was already playing. The center of the room was cleared for dancing. At the end opposite the stage were tables laden with food and punch bowls.

When Natalie looked around, she barely recognized her school friends. Without the usual grungy jeans and T-shirts, they all looked so different—more grown-up, she decided.

Twila, still a sophomore, was there with Colby, a teammate of Stick's.

"Hey, whatcha doin' with *this* bozo?" Stick asked her, clapping a hand on his friend's brawny shoulder and eyeing her appreciatively.

Twila's scarlet dress was stunningly dramatic against her velvety brown skin, Natalie thought. The girl smiled at them, looking pleased and very mature.

Scanning the crowd, Natalie saw Katlyn coming in the door. She was wearing a white strapless dress, its skirt full and foamy. It looked great with her dark hair and coloring, Natalie thought. She braced herself for the sight of Scott, sure to be right behind her. But Katlyn's escort was someone Natalie had never seen before—an older college guy, she figured.

She wondered where Scott could be—why he wasn't here—but at least she was relieved that he wasn't with Katlyn. She shrugged it off and decided to relax and enjoy herself.

It was easy. Stick was at his clownish best, Ruthie as loony as ever, and their combined antics kept

Natalie in stitches. Stick was even a surprisingly good dancer—despite his two left feet—and Natalie was really surprised when the band struck up the last dance. She couldn't believe how fast the time had passed.

When the evening was over and Stick walked her to the door, he was a perfect gentleman. "Tell Amy she has a really great sister. Thanks for going with me, Natalie. I appreciate it."

"It was fun, Stick. And I'll thank Amy for *both* of us."

When Natalie walked in, her dad was home from work, still wearing his prison officer's uniform—gray slacks, navy blazer, light blue shirt, and maroon tie. He whistled when he saw her, then spoiled it by saying, "You look a lot like your mother when she was young."

"Who's calling who *old*?" Jill walked into the living room with a wicked gleam in her eye.

"I meant 'younger,'" Jim amended. "Didn't I, Natalie?"

"You *better*!" Jill threatened, her arm raised to deliver a playful swat.

He grabbed her wrist and gently pulled her into his lap.

For an instant, Natalie caught a glimpse of her mom and dad in their dating years. Her dad—strong and handsome and romantic; her mom—hair pulled back into a ponytail, face all fresh and beautiful.

Natalie gave them a quick update on the prom, then excused herself to go to her room. Standing in front of the mirror, she studied her reflection, wondering if Scott would have approved. *Stop that!* she scolded herself. She might as well resign herself to the fact that her one date with Scott was just exactly that—one special evening. Now it was over. It would be pure stupidity to keep hoping he might ask her out again.

She unzipped her dress and stepped out of it, hanging it carefully in the closet before pulling on a nightshirt. She opened her jewelry box and took out the little white dove, cradling it in the palm of her hand.

After turning off the lamp on her nightstand, Natalie walked over to the window. Looking out over the quiet neighborhood with its sleepy houses, she noticed a few lights still winking in some of the windows. She knew all the people who lived in those houses. Most of them were good Christian people.

Then she opened her hand and looked at the white dove. Andy and Stephanie were right. Symbols were important. She closed her eyes and whispered a prayer, "Lord, it's pretty obvious—even to me—that I shouldn't care too much for a boy I barely know, and that I *should* care about Katlyn—even though it's hard to like her. Help me show them your kind of love and friendship. . . ."

For a moment, Natalie felt the weight of her failure to be loving toward others. Then, looking up at the starlit sky, she lightly clasped the little white dove. "I can't do it by myself, Lord. But with your help, I promise to try."

Saturday was stifling hot, with barely a breeze blowing. Then the air-conditioner went out. The repairman couldn't possibly get to their house before the first of the week, Jill told them when she hung up the phone.

Sunday was worse, and the Ainsworths gave in and let the girls go to the public swimming pool. They all got too much sun, which made matters worse, and by evening, everyone was grouchy.

To cool off, they went to McDonald's for supper. "The car's air-conditioned, too," Jill reminded them.

"Maybe it'll rain," Natalie said hopefully on the way home.

Her mom shrugged. "Not according to the weather forecast," she said. "We'll just have to sit in front of the fan."

"I'm going up to my room to read," Natalie announced as soon as they returned.

"And I've got to hit the books, too," Jill said. "I've got a biology test tomorrow night. Would someone please explain why, at my age, I have to study biology just to get a degree in English?"

"Why, Mom—what is it you're always telling us?" Amy asked. "Expand your mind! Explore the world of interesting subjects. . . ."

"Well," Jill hedged with a sheepish grin, "I guess you're right. But I'm not as young as I once was."

Natalie grinned. "Am I hearing right? Did I just hear our mother admit she was getting old?"

"It's heatstroke," Jill joked, fanning herself with her hand. "I'd better go take a bath first. Maybe it'll help."

109

But it wasn't much cooler by bedtime. Natalie tossed and turned, staring out the open window. Occasionally she saw a distant flash—probably heat lightning—but there was no breeze.

Most of the time, she was glad to be in her attic room over the garage. It was peaceful here, away from the rest of the family. But with the air-conditioning out and no breeze stirring, it was the hottest place in the house.

———

Natalie awoke on Monday morning, her sweaty hair plastered to her head. She took a quick shower and left her hair damp, hoping that would help keep her cool.

When she went downstairs, the kitchen felt stuffy, even with the doors and windows open. Everyone else had finished breakfast, but nobody was saying much. It took too much effort. The girls seemed to be walking around in slow motion, and Jill hadn't even dressed yet.

Natalie grabbed a cereal bowl, filled it, then opened the refrigerator door and reached for the milk, standing in the welcome blast of cold air.

"Close that door, Natalie," her dad scolded, coming in from the hall. "You're cooling the whole outdoors."

"Sorry, Dad." She obeyed reluctantly. When was this heat wave going to break? They were all on edge and cranky.

Hoping to lighten the mood, she made a feeble joke. "We're really going to hate to leave you two here while we go to our nice, air-conditioned school."

No one laughed.

———

"Sorry to leave you kids here while I drive to Carterville in an air-conditioned car and take an exam in an air-conditioned classroom," Jill rubbed it in that evening.

"Paying me back for this morning, aren't you?" Natalie said.

A little gust of wind came through the door. Amy noticed it first. "Hey, did you feel that?"

"Promises, promises," Natalie complained. "It's been heat lightning for two nights now, but there hasn't been a drop of rain."

"There's some bad weather north of us, but nothing like that seems to be headed our way," their mom said. She looked out, studying the sky. "Still clear. Might be a cloud in the distance. If it storms, just don't use the phone. That is, unless there's an emergency. And be careful of electric—"

"Mom!" Natalie interrupted. "How many times have I done this?"

"Ohhhh, a dozen or so." Jill sighed. "Sorry to nag, honey. That's what moms do best, I suppose."

"Worry about your biology test, not about us," Amy said. "Natalie knows how to manage. She just leaves us alone and lets us do our own thing."

Natalie gave her sister a murderous look. "Amy, Mom's going to believe you."

Jill waved her hand helplessly. "Look, you two, it's after five. I'm outta here."

"Good luck on your test!" they called after her.

As soon as their mom had backed out of the drive, Natalie got busy. "Okay, you guys, it's bath time."

"I don't need one," Rose argued.

Natalie frowned, sniffing the air. "Have you been playing with Pongo?"

Rose nodded.

"Shooo!" Amy held her nose. "She smells like a dog!"

Rose bared her teeth, growled, and ran for Amy, chasing her around the living room and down the hall.

"Why aren't *you* giving me any trouble, Sarah?" Natalie asked her sister, who was curled up in a chair reading a book.

Sarah looked up innocently. "I guess it's because I'm perfect."

She grinned, but Natalie thought her color didn't look quite right. She walked over and felt her sister's head. It seemed clammy and awfully warm. "Why don't you go cool off with a bath, Sarah?"

Without a word of protest, Sarah put down her book and headed for the bathroom, just as Amy and Rose ran back into the room, panting with exertion.

The phone rang. Amy ran for it.

"For you, Nat," Amy said, breathless, "and hurry up. I'm expecting a call."

"You're always expecting a call," Natalie returned and took the receiver. Probably Ruthie. She had said something about needing help with a math problem. "Hello?"

"Natalie?" came a hesitant male voice.

"Yes. This is Natalie."

There was a pause. Then, "I need to ask you a favor."

"Scott?"

Eight

"Natalie, this is Scott Lambert. I know this is going to sound weird, but could you go with me . . . somewhere?"

He couldn't be asking for a date! "What did you have in mind?"

"To see Cissy. She's got some . . . problems."

"Well, Dad's working and Mom's at school. I . . . I don't know—"

"Sorry. I shouldn't have asked. I just thought maybe you could help."

He sounded really down. "What's going on, Scott?"

He sighed heavily. "It's kind of a long story. But I've got to go to Cissy. It's pretty urgent."

"Well, look," Natalie said quickly, sensing his concern, "maybe I could get Ruthie to come over and stay with the girls."

Scott seemed relieved. "I wouldn't ask if it weren't really serious, Nat. I mean, my cousin's whole life is about to go down the drain."

"Okay . . . if you really think I could help. . . ."

Natalie wasn't so sure. Why would Cissy Stiles need *her*?

"Be there in a jiff," he said hurriedly and hung up.

Ruthie was more than thrilled when Natalie called. But she had to get permission first. She came back to the phone, breathless as usual. "Mom's at a meeting, but Dad said I could go, and even told me to take his car! Monster already has his jammies on, and I think Dad's about ready to tie him down for the night, so I'll see you in a sec." And she was gone.

Natalie had to laugh in spite of the possible seriousness of the situation. Ruthie always put a humorous twist on things—even bigger-than-life things—like Scott Lambert and the Junior Prom!

Hurrying, Natalie fixed a quick snack for the girls, put Amy in charge of bath time, and changed into clean jeans and a fresh tank top. Too bad there wasn't time to put on some makeup, she thought, grimacing at her reflection in the mirror. At the last minute, she pinned on the little white dove.

Ruthie arrived just as Scott pulled up to the curb and honked his horn. *Good thing Mom and Dad aren't here!* Natalie decided as she let Ruthie in and waved at Scott. She could just hear them now: *Gentlemen come to the door.*

But Scott had implied that this was an emergency. Her parents would understand. At least, she sure hoped they would!

Leaving instructions for Ruthie, Natalie stepped out the front door and felt a blast of cool air. The wind slammed the screen door shut behind her and another gust whipped her hair into her face. Pushing back the flyaway strands with both hands, she ran down the walk to the car.

With his left arm braced on the steering wheel, Scott leaned across to hold the passenger door open for her. She slid into the front seat.

"Wow! That wind is ferocious!" she said, struggling to close the door. Looking out the window, she saw dark clouds scudding across the sky. "Looks as if a storm's brewing."

"Dad mentioned something earlier about a tornado watch." Scott frowned. "If you don't want to go with me, I wouldn't blame you."

Natalie shrugged. "Tornado watches and high winds are just part of our life around here."

He looked a little skeptical but pulled away from the curb. "You ever been in one?"

"Close. We have warnings all the time, especially in the spring." Seeing Scott's concerned face, pale in the eerie light, she wondered what Cissy's problem could be. "What's going on?"

He took a deep breath. "Cissy's parents are away for the evening," he said. "She's waiting for Ron to come get her. . . . They're going to elope."

Natalie's mouth flew open. "Elope?"

He nodded. "I know it's insane, but she's determined to go through with it."

Natalie hardly knew what to say. "B-but why don't they wait till school's out? I mean, she graduates in only a few weeks. . . ."

Scott was shaking his head. "Her parents would never agree to that. They say she has to go to college before she even thinks about getting married."

117

"Is she in love with him?"

Scott tightened his grip on the steering wheel as a gust of wind rocked the car. "Oh, I guess so, but that's not the real reason she wants to marry him. She has her heart set on going to acting school, and her parents won't let her. So, she figures she'll just get married and do as she pleases."

"But how would they ever make it—financially, I mean? Cissy doesn't have a job, and Ron's still in college. . . ."

The set of Scott's jaw betrayed his concern. "That's just it. That girl has no idea where money comes from."

Do you? Natalie wondered as he drove into Garden Acres. Not many high-school guys owned a new sports car, or lived in a big home in the most exclusive section of town.

"What do you want me to do, Scott?" Natalie asked uncertainly. What in the world *could* she do for Cissy Stiles—the girl who had everything?

Scott turned in at a long drive bordered by manicured shrubs, then parked at the side of a two-story white Georgian mansion with a pilaster-flanked front entry.

"I don't see any sign of Ron yet," Scott observed as he parked behind the Audi, the car Natalie had seen Cissy driving many times. "I just hope we're not too late."

With that thought, they picked up their pace as they hurried toward the front door.

Scott tried the brass knob, but the door was locked. He rang the bell and pounded on the solid oak panel with his fist. "Cissy, open up! I know you're in there."

"If you've got someone with you, I'm not letting you in, Scott Lambert. I told you that when you left. I'll . . . do something." Her ominous tone was unmistakable.

"It's only Natalie," Scott called.

Natalie shook off the sting in that remark and concentrated, instead, on the distress in the other girl's voice. "She really sounds upset, Scott. Maybe I'd better stay in the car."

Scott pounded harder. "Come on, Cissy," he pleaded. "We'll only stay for a minute. We just want to talk."

There was a frightening pause before Cissy spoke again. "Ron will be here any time now. Then I'm leaving."

"I know, I know," Scott said soothingly. "But we're about to blow away out here!"

They leaned against the door, trying to avoid the driving wind. Turning her head, Natalie gasped, feeling the breath sucked from her body.

She heard the lock slip and, when Scott turned the knob this time, the door opened and they stumbled into the foyer.

Cissy turned away defiantly. A suitcase was waiting near the door.

"Well, at least sit down till Ron gets here, Cissy," Scott insisted. "Natalie has something she'd like to say." He turned in her direction, an unspoken plea in his eyes.

"Really, Scott, couldn't you have done better than Natalie Ainsworth? The police? The FBI? A reporter from *Inside Edition?* Do you really think Miss Goody-Two-Shoes can talk me out of this?"

Scott shot Natalie an apologetic look.

But it really didn't matter to her. What *did* matter was that Cissy's eyes were red and puffy and that she appeared to be on the edge. Besides, being called goody-two-shoes was really not all that bad. From dealing with her three sisters, Natalie knew that insults were sometimes used to cover up pain. And Cissy Stiles was obviously hurting big time.

"You're right, Cissy," Natalie said honestly. "If you've really made up your mind to ruin your life, no one can stop you. I know *I* can't. Who knows, I might even agree with you if I understood why you were doing this."

Cissy glared at her. "Do you think I'm stupid, Natalie Ainsworth? That I don't know what you're trying to pull?"

If looks could kill, Natalie thought, *I'd be flat on my back.* Her own gaze didn't waver. "I only want to help," she said quietly.

To Natalie's surprise, Cissy dropped her head. "I'm sorry. I just feel like striking out sometimes. It's my parents . . . they won't listen to me. They don't understand. . . ."

"They're just trying to protect you."

"Oh, come off it, Natalie! I don't need protecting! I'm perfectly capable of taking care of myself!"

A car squealed to a stop outside.

"That's Ron," Cissy said.

"Cissy," Natalie began, desperately stalling for time. *What would Jesus say at a time like this?* "God wants us to obey our parents. . . ."

"But there comes a time when we have to make our own decisions," the older girl argued. "I'm nearly eighteen, you know."

"We're supposed to respect our parents no matter how old we are, Cissy. And since your parents are opposed to what you want to do, maybe you should wait a while. You have time, and running away is not the answer. Why not try talking to them again?"

"My parents won't listen to anyone. They think they know everything!" The doorbell rang. Cissy headed for it.

Scott touched her arm as she passed by. "Please don't go."

Natalie could think of nothing else to say. Impulsively, she reached up and unclasped her pin. "Wait a minute, Cissy."

"I'm not waiting—not another second!" she tossed over her shoulder on her way to open the door for Ron.

Natalie kept talking. "When people get married, they receive presents. Here." She held out her hand, fist closed over the tiny pin.

Cissy hesitated, looking skeptical, as if fearing Natalie might try to grab her arm and force her to stay. Slowly, Cissy stretched out her hand. Natalie lay the little white dove in the girl's open palm. "I hold on to this when I need God's help."

Cissy barely glanced at the gift but accepted it. Tired of waiting, Ron let himself in, picked up Cissy's suitcase, then hurried her out the door.

Scott and Natalie stood in the doorway, watching the couple—arms around each other—fight the wind all the way to the car.

Once Cissy was safely belted into the passenger's seat, she bent her head, her shoulders shaking. Natalie knew she was sobbing.

"I'm sorry I couldn't do anything to stop her," Natalie said as they drove away.

Scott slumped in dejection. "Well, thanks anyway. It was worth a try." He closed the door, went into the large living room, and sunk down onto the plush sofa.

Natalie sat down in a chair opposite him. "Do you think you should contact her parents?"

"They're having dinner with friends. Some kind of business contact, Cissy said. But she wouldn't say where." Scott raked his hand through his hair. "She was all set to take off right after they left the house."

"But she told *you*."

He nodded. "We're pretty close. Cissy waited for a night when the maid was off, then wrote a note to her parents. I'm supposed to be sure they find it. When I begged her not to do this, she got frantic. That's why I called you, thinking she might listen. I know she respects you a lot."

That was a surprise to Natalie. "Maybe you should call the police."

He looked distressed. "I can't do that, Natalie. Cissy's not a criminal . . . she's just mixed up."

"Could *your* parents talk to her?"

He hesitated. "My dad's making rounds at the hospital tonight."

There was no mention of his mother. Natalie wondered about that, but simply said, "What about your aunt, Mrs. Brysen? Should she be told?"

He shook his head firmly. "Not *her*."

A strong gust of wind rattled the windowpanes and diverted their attention. Natalie frowned. "I'd better go home before this storm gets any worse."

———

They didn't talk much on the way back. The wind picked up and clawed at the car like some kind of monster, threatening to lift it off the street. Giant oak branches writhed and twisted convulsively. The roar seemed to intensify, then dropped to a frightening silence.

In one of the calmer moments, Scott glanced over at Natalie. "What was that you gave Cissy?"

Natalie wasn't sure she wanted to tell him. Not yet. What if he didn't understand? What if he thought she was some kind of fanatic? "A white dove pin," she said a little reluctantly.

"I've seen several of those around lately."

He seemed interested. Encouraged, she went on. "They have a special meaning. If you'd like to come in," she said when he pulled up in front of the house, "I can tell you all about it."

"Your parents wouldn't mind? I've probably already gotten you in trouble."

Natalie glanced at the car clock. "They're very understanding. And Mom's class isn't over until eight o'clock."

He turned off the engine and got out. Natalie still wasn't sure what that meant. *Does he want to be with me?* she wondered. *Is he really interested in hearing about the dove pin? Or is he just waiting until the wind dies down?*

———

"Hi, Scott," Ruthie said, greeting them at the door. "Nat, Dad called and said a wingding of a storm's coming in. So I gotta scoot before it hits."

"Go! And thanks for staying with the girls. Call me when you get home."

Ruthie's big brown eyes pled for an explanation.

"Later," Natalie promised as she shoved her friend out the door. "And thanks again."

"Anytime—oooooh!" Ruthie squealed, her voice swallowed up in the roar of the wind and the crash of thunder.

"Maybe we shouldn't have let her go," Scott said with a frown as they shut the door.

"Oh, she can beat the storm." Natalie laughed lightly, trying to cover her own concern. "She may not be the world's best driver, but she only lives a block and a half away."

Scott's answering chuckle seemed forced, Natalie thought. Their eyes swung to the TV, where a special report had interrupted the program in progress. In one corner of the screen a dark funnel cloud was depicted in a small yellow box.

Amy punched the remote to turn up the volume. Sarah and Rose were sitting on the couch, legs drawn up under them, watching the set, wide-eyed.

"This is a tornado warning. I repeat, not a *watch*, but a *warning*. The following counties must take note and stay tuned for further reports." An alphabetical listing scrolled across the screen.

Tornado warning! Natalie knew what that meant. A *watch* was issued when conditions were right for a tornado. A *warning* meant a tornado was imminent. Probably a twister had already been spotted somewhere in the viewing area!

Scott looked worried. "Do they always say that?"

Natalie glanced at her sisters, who had been glued to the TV but were now watching her to see what her answer would be. She was saved temporarily by the meteorologist's next words.

"If a tornado is sighted, go to a basement or take cover in a hallway or closet. The inner supporting walls will help protect you against flying objects." Outside walls, Natalie knew, were most vulnerable, and a damaged roof could cave in under pressure. "Avoid windows because of the danger of flying glass." Again and again came the staccato announcement: "This is a tornado warning! This is a tornado warning!"

Natalie had the feeling that this was different from any warning she had ever experienced before. They'd better get busy. "Okay, get the mattresses, pillows, and flashlight," she ordered, recalling their last tornado scare. "And crack your bedroom windows. Mom's too." At least, Natalie thought, with the air-conditioning out, most of the windows had already been opened to let in whatever breeze was stirring. It was important to equalize the pressure in the house, she knew.

Scott was still listening to the weather report. At Natalie's last words, he turned. "What can I do to help?"

"How about making sure the windows are up in the kitchen and bathroom?" she said on her way out the door to the stairs.

He seemed puzzled. "You mean closed, don't you?"

"No," she took time to explain. "Mom says if the house is closed up during a tornado, it could implode."

"Oh, fall in. The opposite of *explode*, right?"

"Right. Now everyone go do your thing, then get into the hallway."

Natalie saw an impish gleam in Scott's eyes. "Do we have to follow school procedure?"

They all shrieked with laughter, easing the tension. "No way!" shouted Amy. "You try that, buddy, and you're out the door!"

Just then a great sheet of lightning flashed against the living room window, and the TV popped loudly and flickered. The girls squealed, and Natalie jumped. Scott clapped his hands together, probably to hide the fact that he, too, had been startled. "Okay, you heard your sister. Now, move!"

To Natalie's surprise, they scrambled. "I'd better check my room," she said.

"I'll get the windows downstairs." He caught Natalie's eye and mouthed, "Hurry!"

As frightening as the storm was, she began to feel a sense of adventure.

She ran upstairs. Her front window was open, but she took a moment to raise the side one. With her hands on the window frame, she stood transfixed, watching the storm.

On the horizon, sharp flashes of light—like jagged teeth—seemed to bite and tear as they streaked through what appeared to be a great black sheet rolling across the sky toward her. The wind had stopped blowing. Everything was absolutely still. Scary! She was accustomed to wind, but she'd heard about the "lull before the storm." What had her mom said? That before a tornado struck, it sucked up all the air? Did that account for the heaviness in her chest?

Something caught her eye. Something moving out of the black sheet. A funnel cloud! She had never seen one before, except in pictures. It spun forward, faster and faster.

"Natalieeeee!"

Amy's loud summons spurred Natalie to action. She shoved the window up and dashed down the stairs.

Standing in the doorway between the living room and hallway, with the voice of the newscaster rising to a crescendo, she looked around at the terrified girls. They had dragged in the mattresses from Rose's and Sarah's twin beds. Blankets and pillows were piled on the floor.

"I've got to get Pongo," Rose said fearfully

"No, you can't go out in this wind," Natalie cautioned. "He'll be okay under the back step." She prayed it would be true.

Scott appeared beside Natalie. "Windows are up," he said thinly, his face about the color of the sheet on Rose's bed. Natalie guessed that he, too, had noticed the strange-looking sky.

The TV announcer repeated the warning, his tone rising as the light outside the window turned an ominous yellow-green. "There have been sightings and reports of several touchdowns. All of Williamson County is under a tornado warning. Take cover immediately! I repeat—"

"Down!" Natalie commanded.

The girls hit the floor.

"I want by Natalie," Rose whimpered.

Sarah and Amy lunged for their pillows, face down, and pulled the mattress over them. Natalie helped Rose with her pillow, then spread two more for herself and Scott.

Suddenly the area tornado alarm sounded. *Braak! Braak! Braak!—Braak! Braak! Braak!—Braak! Braak! Braak!*

They all screamed as the terrifying noise split the air. It was much worse than the alarm at school. Surely everyone for miles around could hear it.

"Come on!" Natalie motioned to Scott and stretched out next to Rose.

Following Natalie's lead, he dropped down beside her and pulled the mattress over the three of them. Braced on their forearms, heads and shoulders propped against the mattresses, all of them resembled great, hulking beasts.

Braak! Braak! Braak!—Braak! Braak! Braak!— Braak! Braak! Braak!

On and on the signal blared. Natalie *felt* the sound grating on her nerves like the scraping of fingernails against sandpaper. That sound was more frightening than the TV warning or even the black funnel spiraling closer.

Amy flicked on the flashlight.

"Better save those batteries in case we need them later," Natalie cautioned.

Amy tossed her the flashlight. Natalie turned it off and stashed it under her pillow.

"I want Mommy." Any minute now, Rose would be wailing.

"She's safe at school, honey," Natalie spoke up, hoping to reassure her little sister. *At least I hope she's safe and not out on the road in this storm!*

Braak! Braak! Br—!

In midblast, the raucous signal stopped.

The TV gulped and died.

The shadowy shapes in the hallway were swallowed up in complete darkness.

No one made a sound.

The silence that throbbed in Natalie's ears was somehow more foreboding than the warning blasts. She heard her own labored breathing. *Is it because I'm scared, or because I'm next to Scott?*

"Is this the usual routine?" Scott whispered close to her ear.

"No," she admitted under her breath, "it's never felt like this before. I hope Ruthie got home okay."

The house began to shudder and creak. "I keep thinking about Cissy and Ron," Scott said quietly.

Natalie had also wondered about them. Where were they? Had they made it out of Garden City before the storm struck? "We'd better pray."

"For us, too?" Rose's little voice was pitched even higher than usual.

"Yes, honey. Let's hold hands . . . if we can find one another."

All five felt their way through the inky blackness until they found a hand. Holding on for dear life, they squeezed their eyes shut while Natalie prayed, asking God's protection for those who were out in the storm— Ruthie, Ron and Cissy, maybe even their mom. Dad, Natalie knew, would be working until dawn.

A sudden roll of thunder shook the house. Great bursts of wind beat furiously against the walls, wailing mournfully around the eaves as if disappointed that it couldn't get in. A low drumroll began somewhere in the distance, vibrating the earth and building in intensity until it sounded like a locomotive bearing down on them. Then it was joined by more trains, it seemed—whistling, moaning, roaring, while things banged, crashed, and cracked about them.

Natalie heard Rose's sobs and felt her trembling body jammed against hers. Or was it her own body trembling? She managed to free one arm from the cumbersome mattress and drape it across her little sister's back.

Then there was the sound of hundreds of trains—maybe thousands—thumping against the walls, crashing into the house. With a mighty roar and a shattering, splintering noise, one of the trains broke through at last. The living room?

Terror-stricken, the girls screamed. Rose clutched furiously at Natalie, who tried her best to console her little sister. The wind whistled through the hallway—a wild thing—trying to rip the protective covering from them, to steal the very breath from their bodies. For a moment Natalie almost panicked. Then she felt a calming touch. *Scott's* hand!

"Our Father, who is in heaven . . ." he began, lifting his voice above the din of the storm. One by one, the girls joined in, concentrating on the comforting words.

Then, almost as suddenly as the commotion began, the trains seemed to be moving away. The deafening roar ceased. The silence wasn't as scary this time. In the stillness, they could hear the gentle pattering of rain, though it sounded very close. They lifted sweaty faces to the now-chilly air. It smelled fresh and clean and cool.

An eerie light filtered in through the doorway from the living room. It wasn't even dark yet, Natalie realized. It was the storm that had turned the sky darker than a moonless night.

"Is everyone okay?" she whispered, looking around at the gray, expressionless faces.

They shifted a little, stretching tentatively.

"Can I take the mattress off now?" Scott asked politely.

At his question and the ridiculous sight they all made, all four girls burst out laughing. They hooted and howled until the tears rained down their cheeks. Scott grinned sheepishly, then joined in the riotous laughter.

Still on their knees, Natalie's sisters slid out from their steamy hideouts and struggled to stand, feeling for bruises. While they were preoccupied, Scott reached over and took Natalie's hand again, squeezing it gently before helping her to her feet.

Reluctant for the moment to end, she turned toward the dusky light at the doorway. "I think it's over," she said, but she didn't sound too sure. *Was* it over?

Was her mom safe at school, or had she been caught out in the storm? Where were Ron and Cissy? Had Ruthie made it home okay?

And . . . what would they find in the living room? If it was still standing when they got there!

Nine

Walking single file, the five storm survivors at the Ainsworth house crept to the door and peered into the living room. The murky light revealed a huge, jagged hole in the picture window where a board had penetrated like a sword. One side of the drapery was torn and dangled from its rod.

"We'll need the flashlight," Natalie said.

Someone found it for her, and she swept the room with the beam of light, revealing shards of glass scattered across the floor. One lamp was overturned. But there was no other visible damage.

A distant siren pierced the quickly darkening night. Rose cried out and grabbed Natalie's arm.

"It's okay. It's probably just an ambulance or a fire truck." Natalie winced at her poor choice of words. That wouldn't make Rose—or anyone else—feel much better.

"There's not as much glass by the door," Scott said, changing the subject. "I'll try to see what's going on outside."

"Stay back," Natalie instructed the girls and shone

the light on the floor ahead as she and Scott picked a path to the door.

But her sisters were right behind. As soon as the door was open, Pongo, who had broken his chain and run around to the front of the house, leaped into Rose's arms, yapping with excitement. She cuddled him close, crooning his name over and over while he licked her face ecstatically.

The wailing sirens seemed to be getting closer. Night had settled in now, and the neighbors were beginning to come to their doors—some with lanterns, others with flashlights. They called to one another, inquiring about the status of households. Apparently no one had been injured in the immediate neighborhood. But they'd have to wait until daylight to see how much damage had been done.

When Natalie and Scott made an inspection of the interior of the house, they found almost everything intact. Except for the living room window, only small objects had been blown about and a few dishes broken in the kitchen, but no major casualties.

Natalie's sense of relief was soon replaced with dread. "I should call Ruthie." She made her way cautiously to the phone. The line was dead.

"I have a cellular phone in my car. We could use that," Scott offered.

"Be careful out there," Natalie cautioned, handing him the flashlight.

He gave her an appreciative glance. "Yeah. Thanks." Using the flash to scope out the littered walkway, Scott stepped gingerly around sections of roofing that had blown off someone's roof and odds and ends that had been strewn about. From her vantage point at the front door, Natalie thought the scene resembled pictures of war-torn areas she had seen on television. She could see Scott speaking to several of her neighbors before he returned with the phone.

"Everyone out there seems all right," he said. "But they believe the tornado hit somewhere near here."

Natalie cocked her head, listening. "The sirens do seem to be getting closer." She shone the light on the phone while Scott punched in the numbers.

No use. He couldn't get through to anyone—not Ruthie, or the college, or the hospital. He tried Cissy's house. No answer. "Aunt Martha has a cellular phone," he recalled, frowning in exasperation, "but I can't remember the number."

"You think Mom's okay?" Rose asked in a trembly little voice, holding tightly to the squirming puppy.

"Of course she is!" Natalie pulled them both close, accidentally turning off the flashlight and plunging them into pitch-black darkness.

Glancing out the window, she noticed a faint glow from some of the windows. "Candles! We can light candles!"

Scott was all for it. "Great! Then maybe we can clean up some of the mess before your parents get home."

Flicking the flashlight back on, Natalie led the way into the kitchen, where she found an emergency cache of candles and matches. She and Scott lit several, and Amy and Sarah placed them in holders and set them in strategic places—the coffee table and a couple of end tables in the living room. Then they all pitched in—everyone except Rose, who was still holding Pongo—and began carefully picking up some of the larger pieces of glass.

When they had filled the kitchen trash can, Natalie spread blankets over the carpet to protect them from the minute slivers they couldn't see in the flickering candle flame.

By now the sirens were so loud that it almost sounded as if the vehicles were careening onto their street, intermittent flashes of swirling blue light marking the route. A commotion could be heard only a short distance away.

Then someone was shouting, "Natalie!"

Out of the darkness, another circle of light appeared, followed by Ruthie on the other end of a flash. Mr. Ryan and Justin trailed behind. Natalie had never been so glad to see anyone in her entire life!

"You girls okay?" Ruthie's dad wanted to know.

"We're fine!" Natalie assured him, though she was tempted to tell him how scared she had been. *If Scott had not been here . . .*

Then everyone was talking at once, giving their version of the storm.

"My car was trashed—after I made it home, that is," Ruthie explained. "There's a log sticking out of the top of it."

"*Your* car?" Mr. Ryan lifted his brow quizzically.

Even in the glow of the candles, Natalie could see Ruthie's face turning almost the shade of her hair.

"Well . . . *Dad's* car," she corrected herself, looking askance at her father.

"We couldn't have driven over anyway," Mr. Ryan

went on. "There's too much debris in the streets."

"I saw the tornado coming—this big, black funnel rolling across the sky," Ruthie said. "It was so weird."

"Dad had to run out and jerk her inside," Justin said, his freckles shining like copper pennies in the candlelight.

"I couldn't move," Ruthie explained. "I felt like I was in some kind of trance. But I wasn't scared!"

"Well, *I* was!" Mr. Ryan admitted.

Ruthie shrugged. "Well, maybe I was, too—a little. We finally climbed into the crawl space under the house."

"I wanted to watch," Justin pouted.

"Your mom's not home yet?" Ruthie asked.

Natalie shook her head.

"Mine, either."

"I'm sure they're both fine." Mr. Ryan was reassuring. "This was Molly's day to volunteer at the hospital, and they do have a shelter there and an emergency power source. But we need to get back to the house in case we hear from her."

"I'll stay around to keep an eye on things here, sir," Scott volunteered. "Do you think we could help in any way?"

"Not yet, son," Mr. Ryan said. "The police will secure the area until emergency crews can assess the situation. The first priority will be to determine the damage and set up rescue operations. When they can, they'll let people in the community know what they can do to help. But I advise you to stay in the house for now."

Right after the Ryans left, Scott's phone rang.

"Answer it!" Amy yelled.

He grabbed for it. "It's Aunt Martha," he mouthed around the receiver.

Quickly he filled his aunt in on where he had been during the storm and told her that Cissy and Ron had left together just before the tornado struck. "Aunt Martha's in her car, using her cellular phone," he told Natalie and the girls. "She said that just before the electricity went off, a newscaster reported a tornado rolling right over the highway, headed toward the western part of Garden City. There doesn't seem to be any damage in Garden Acres, but emergency vehicles are using the highway, so traffic is blocked off. She's going to try to reach the hospital and let Dad know I'm all right."

You can say that again! Natalie thought, giving Scott an admiring glance. She went to the front door, hoping to shut out the sound of sirens screaming through the night. But before she did, she noticed that the air—much cooler now—was stirring up a gentle breeze.

How quickly things could change. A few days ago, her biggest worry had been whether Scott Lambert would ask her to the Junior Prom. Now, that seemed so trivial compared with all the people out there who might be hurt, or homeless . . . or worse.

To lift their spirits while waiting for some kind of news from Jill Ainsworth, Natalie forced a cheery note into her voice. "Anyone hungry?"

"Yeah, Pongo's probably *starved*!" Rose said.

Natalie picked up a candle and led the way into the kitchen.

"Let's drink milk, not Coke," she suggested, setting the half-gallon jug on the table. "We don't know when the electricity will come back on, and the milk could spoil. And we can make some peanut-butter-and-jelly sandwiches."

Rose took the flashlight to the back door and shone it around. "I don't see Pongo's bowl anywhere." She shut the door, found a bowl in the cupboard, and spooned some dog food into it.

Natalie grimaced but decided not to say anything. What were a few doggie germs after all they'd been through?

"Dad's not scared of anything," Sarah said, digging into the peanut butter and spreading it on a piece of bread. "He says if a tornado hits, there's nothing you can do anyway, so he lies on the bed and takes a nap during a watch."

"Remember what Mom used to do when we were little?" Amy asked mischievously.

The girls snickered.

Natalie shot them a disapproving look. "Now don't you tell Scott that!"

Scott reached for the bread. "Oh, I think I'd like to hear it," he said, egging them on.

Amy put the grape jelly and some knives on the table. "When we were younger," she began over Natalie's protests, "we had youth beds with foam mattresses. Some little person—I won't call her by name . . ."

"You better not! Sic her, Pongo!" Rose shoved the puppy toward Amy, but he only gave Rose another juicy lick before returning to his bowl.

"Anyway," Amy continued, "this little one would occasionally wet the mattress—and when Mom put it over us during a warning, we were too busy holding our noses to worry about a little old tornado!"

Everyone laughed, except Rose, who kept a straight face as she went over to the sink and washed her hands. Then, weary of her sisters' ribbing, she came to the table and accepted the sandwich Natalie had made for her.

"Another time," Sarah took up the role of story-teller, "we were in the playroom when the wind started whistling. We crouched under the Ping-Pong table and watched the storm through the window. Pretty soon, we could see someone's roof flying by—"

"Turned out to be *ours*!" Amy finished, taking a seat across from her sister. "That wind was so ferocious it bent Mrs. Golding's TV antenna over double."

"And it tore off a big limb in Flashpullers' yard and split the trunk in half," Natalie remembered as she made herself a sandwich.

"There was hail, too," Sarah added, "the size of golf balls. It made huge dents in the cars. Dad said it looked like they all had giant-sized chicken pox."

This brought a giggle from Rose.

Funny how the girls were competing for Scott's attention, Natalie thought. They seemed determined to outdo one another. But she was just as pleased as they were that he had decided to stay for a while.

"I've never been in a tornado before," he said after a big gulp of milk. "But I was in an earthquake in California once."

All heads swiveled in his direction.

"What was it like?" Natalie asked.

"I was in the supermarket with my dad when the

building started shaking. Then the groceries started falling off the shelves—jelly jars, pickles, catsup. Cans were hopping all over the place. It was like things had sprouted legs. Soda pop bottles burst and fizzed like geysers."

"We had an earthquake here," Amy put in. "Tell him, Natalie."

"Mom tells it better," Natalie said but launched into the story. Anything was better than waiting for the news of their friends and loved ones who were still missing. "Amy and I were across the street playing. Sarah was in the front yard. Mom was folding laundry in the living room where she could watch Sarah and keep an eye on Rose, who was asleep in her bassinet. Things started shaking. Even the baby's cradle was rocking. Mom didn't know if it was the end of the world or what! She wanted to go get Sarah, but she was afraid to leave baby Rose. So, she stood in the doorway, watching Sarah try to crawl to her, not making much progress because the earth was moving. Mom said the look on her face was priceless! And the baby slept on, rocking away. . . ."

By this time they were all laughing so hard they were about to choke. Suddenly aware of the uncertainty of the moment, Natalie sobered. "Maybe we shouldn't be joking around. Some people out there are really hurting, and we still don't know . . ."

"Well, my dad says laughter is great therapy," Scott spoke up. "It actually helps sick people heal faster"— he grew suddenly serious—"though . . . sometimes . . . it's hard to laugh."

Again Natalie had the feeling that Scott Lambert

had locked something up inside. He really ought to let it out—whatever it was.

Noticing the flame burning low, she glanced at the girls. Their eyelids seemed to be drooping, too, and Rose's head was beginning to nod. "I think you guys better get some sleep. With all the junk on the highway, it may be a while before Mom gets home."

For the first time since she could remember, she didn't get any opposition from her sisters.

———

Long after midnight, Scott and Natalie were still sitting at the kitchen table. When Scott's phone rang again, he grabbed it on the first ring. "Probably Dad or Aunt Martha."

As he listened, his expression grew increasingly grim. After what seemed forever, the conversation ended, and he slowly pushed the antenna into the phone and laid it on the table. Looking up, his gaze met Natalie's. "That was Aunt Martha. . . . They found Ron . . . but not Cissy."

"Found him? Where?"

"He's in the hospital."

"Will he be . . . all right?" The words stuck to the roof of her mouth like peanut butter.

Scott sighed. "Aunt Martha didn't know any details."

Natalie reached over and grasped his hands. How ghostly he looked in the candlelight. His lip seemed to quiver, but maybe that was only because she was looking at him through watery eyes.

He bent his head. She figured he must be praying.

How awful not to know what had happened to his cousin! She might be . . . "We shouldn't think the worst, Scott. She's probably safe somewhere. We've prayed about it. Now we'll just have to trust God."

He smiled faintly. "You're right. Thanks for reminding me." He straightened and drew in a deep breath. "At least Aunt Martha said Cissy's parents got home safely. And Dad will stay at the hospital as long as he's needed."

Natalie understood. "My dad will probably have to work right through the night and early-morning shifts at the prison, too, like he does when there are escapes." She glanced at her watch. "But I'm getting worried about Mom. She should be home by now."

As if on cue, Natalie heard the front screen bang, and her mom calling her name. They met at the kitchen door and fell into each other's arms.

"Is everybody all right here, honey?"

"Yes, Mom. I sent the girls to bed, and I didn't get any static. This has been a long day."

"And how!" Jill Ainsworth sank wearily into the nearest chair.

"Oh, and Scott's been with us the whole time," Natalie rushed to explain. "He really helped out."

Jill reached across the table and patted his hand. "Thanks, Scott. I wouldn't have worried quite so much if I'd known there was a man around the house."

Embarrassed, he ducked his head, but Natalie guessed he felt pretty proud of himself.

"Let me catch my breath and I'll make some coffee," Jill said, then focused on the candle. "I forgot. There's no electricity." She shook her head. "You wouldn't believe what it's like out there."

"Can I get you something cold to drink, Mom?"

"Thanks, honey. Would you get me a Coke while I check on the girls?"

She was back in a moment. "I roused them long enough to kiss them and tell them I'm home. I didn't even throw the dog out. By the way, what's with the living room? Blankets all over."

Natalie and Scott brought her up to date, including Cissy's boyfriend's condition and the fact that Cissy was still missing. Then it was Jill's turn. "We were in no danger at the college, of course. There's a basement and other designated safety areas. But the traffic was tied up for miles on the highway, so we were advised not to try to leave."

"I guess I couldn't even get home if I tried, could I?" Scott asked.

Jill gave him an apologetic glance. "Probably not. Some of the streets are blocked off so traffic won't interfere with the workers. And there are downed trees and debris everywhere. I parked at the elementary school and walked home. People are milling around everywhere. Some are hurt, some still dazed and unable to find their homes." The look on Jill's face was tragic.

"Could you see where it hit, Mom?" Natalie wanted to know.

"Not exactly, but it looks as if there could have been more than one tornado, or it could have struck in several places. The closest is just three blocks away. They're setting up volunteer stations now." She shivered. "You kids were in real danger. I . . . I'm so grateful you're all right. . . ."

There was a long pause as the truth dawned.

Then Jill spoke more briskly. "After I rest a minute more, I'm going over to see what I can do to help. You two better try to get some rest. You'll probably be needed as soon as it's light." She glanced over at Scott. "You don't mind staying just a little longer, do you? I'd feel better knowing the girls are in good hands."

"Oh yes, ma'am," Scott agreed. "I can't make it home anyway. But I don't think I could sleep."

"Well, just stretch out on the couch in the living room and try to rest. You can grab a pillow and a blanket from the hall. And, Natalie, you can use Dad's recliner. I won't be long." Jill finished her Coke and rose, gave Natalie a hug, and picked up her slicker on the way out.

Natalie was a little confused but figured it was okay since it was her mom's idea. Besides, this was an emergency, and she wanted to be near Scott's phone in case anyone called about Cissy.

Retrieving the pillows and blankets, they settled down on the couch and chair across from each other. There was an embarrassing silence before Natalie finally spoke. "Looks like you're stuck with us."

He didn't answer right away. Then, "I really like your family, Natalie. They're great." He studied her for a long moment. "And so are you." With that, he leaned back and closed his eyes.

Natalie could only stare at him, hoping he wouldn't catch her looking. She could hardly believe it! Scott Lambert—every girl's heartthrob—*here*, in *her* house.

Some girls got butterflies around a guy like Scott. But she had experienced thunder, lightning, and killer winds—just like a tornado had roared through her heart!

Ten

It was eight o'clock the next morning before Scott and Natalie opened their eyes again. Jill and Jim Ainsworth were just coming in the front door, stepping carefully on the quilts and blankets still covering the carpet.

Natalie's dad knit his brows in a scowl. "This place looks as if a tornado hit it!"

Her mom was grinning. "But it's still standing!"

Natalie jumped up, then winced, feeling stiff and sore from her night in the recliner. "Dad, this is Scott Lambert. He—"

Jim stuck out his hand. "Oh, I know all about this young man. Appreciate your standing by, son."

Scott rose hurriedly, throwing off the light blanket, and returned the firm grip. "Maybe I should tell you why I was here in the first place, sir. I—"

"There's time for all that. Come on into the kitchen. I bought some sweet rolls on the way home—your favorite, Natalie."

Jill brought the juice and milk—by some miracle, still cool—from the refrigerator, and they sat around the table while Scott related the whole story of Ron and Cissy.

"I don't know what else you could have done," Natalie's mom said sympathetically.

"And I'm proud of you, Natalie, for calling Ruthie to stay with the girls while you tried to help," her dad added. He glanced from Scott to Natalie. "The two of you have come through a real ordeal with flying colors. There's more than one kind of storm in this world."

Natalie shrugged. "Well, we really didn't know we were in danger from a tornado," she replied truthfully. "We just did all the things you taught us, Mom . . . and we prayed a lot." She flashed Scott a smile, then sobered. "But we're really worried about Scott's cousin Cissy. They still haven't found her. We don't know if she and Ron got married—even if they both make it through this, their lives could be changed forever!"

Jim sighed heavily, a grim expression settling over his features. "Well, hon, that's the price we pay for deciding to get married, no matter what our age—"

Jill reached across the table and smacked his arm while he blanched in mock terror, throwing up his hands to defend himself from her blows. Scott grinned at Natalie, who shook her head and looked toward the ceiling.

Actually, Natalie loved these playful moods—her mom and dad pretending to fight while love shone from their eyes. It made her feel warm and secure. Later, she'd be going out to see what damage the tornado had done last night. But it was really comforting to know that she always had a safe place and loving parents to come home to.

Word of the clean-up efforts spread rapidly through the neighborhood. Volunteers would be needed to provide food for the workers, clear rubble and pile it on trucks to be hauled away, and cut and stack wood from fallen trees. Some helpers would be working on site, while others offered their homes as temporary shelters for those still without a place to stay, or cared for children of workers.

While they were making their plans, the rest of the family—including Pongo, still in Rose's arms—came into the kitchen. The girls were glad to see their parents and eager to hear everything.

"Mom will tell you," Jim promised, giving each of them a hug. "I'm going over to see what I can do to help."

"You've been up all night," Jill reminded him. "Why don't you sleep for a couple of hours first?"

"I'm off for the next two days. I'll sleep tonight." He gave her a searching look. "It could have been *our* house—our family."

"I'd like to go with you, sir," Scott offered.

"So would I," said Natalie.

"I want to help, too." That was Amy.

"Unless your mother needs you here," Jim cautioned, giving Jill an inquiring glance.

"I could use Rose and Sarah. We'll gather up some clothes and cooking utensils to take to the church, where they're setting up a center to care for children of victims and volunteers."

Natalie, Amy, their dad, and Scott—after retrieving Scott's video camera from his car—set out on foot.

Walking through the rubble was bad enough, but the site of the actual touchdown—three blocks from the Ainsworth home—was unbelievable.

The houses that were left standing, their roofs blown off, resembled decapitated corpses. Entire trees had penetrated some of the walls and still protruded, like giant toothpicks. Other houses had been reduced to little more than slivers of wood and brick. The wind had leveled them as easily as if they had been made of cardboard.

But this was no toy village. This was for real.

State and local emergency crews were on the scene to direct the clean-up operations. Just about everyone from church was there to help, along with some of the neighbors—Ruthie, Sean, and a few guys Natalie didn't recognize. As the day wore on, the pieces began to fall into place like a huge puzzle. There had been damaging winds in other places throughout the state, but here, a single tornado had been responsible for at least three deadly touchdowns. First, an apartment complex had been completely demolished, leaving several dead. Then the tornado had skipped over an area, swooping down to destroy another neighborhood near the highway before taking one more leap and landing here on this street. The search for casualties had gone on all night long.

"The National Guard was called in to keep looters away," someone said.

Natalie turned to Scott. "How could anyone even *think* of stealing at a time like this?"

"I heard there were some kids about your age out here doing just that," a bystander spoke up. "They pretended to be helping, but it was obvious they were looking for valuables because a couple of them were seen running with sacks in their hands. The way they were operating, they seemed to be part of a gang."

"A gang? Here in Garden City?" Natalie couldn't believe it.

"We hope not!" Jim responded.

The Ministerial Alliance was on hand collecting necessities for the victims and setting up emergency housing. In fact, help had come from counties hundreds of miles away. It was encouraging to see so many people all working together in this crisis—picking up debris, chopping wood, repairing homes, and putting on new roofs.

"Hey, over here! Over here!" an emergency worker shouted.

Natalie turned to look.

The man lifted a bundle from a pile of rubbish and held it high. Just then a baby began to cry, and a young couple stumbled through the debris, their faces streaked with tears. "My baby! My baby!" screamed the woman.

Apparently, the couple had searched for their child all night after the nursery had been blown away from their house. They had almost given up hope that the infant had survived.

At first glance, the child, bound tightly in its blanket, appeared to be okay. At least, the cry was loud enough, Natalie thought. A closer examination by a doctor on the scene revealed only a small scratch on one tiny finger. He sent the couple to a local church, set up to help those with minor injuries, and Natalie saw them hurrying away, their tired faces wreathed in smiles.

———

On the way home, a stunned Jim Ainsworth was shaking his head. "Do you realize that the tornado skipped right over our block?"

"I guess I hadn't given it much thought," Natalie admitted, trudging along between her dad and Scott. "This all still seems so unreal to me."

Jim stopped and stared as if seeing his house for the first time. "I'm sure you were praying when the tornado came through," he said quietly. "I was."

"We did pray . . . a lot," Natalie replied seriously.

"Have you thanked God yet for answering your prayer?"

Natalie looked sheepish. "Guess I forgot that part."

"Let's do it now."

The three of them stood together, holding hands while Jim prayed aloud, thanking the Lord for sparing them and asking that He care for those who had lost loved ones or homes. "Amen," they chorused when he had finished, and Natalie felt the little squeeze Scott gave her hand before releasing it.

As soon as they were inside, Jill told them that Martha Brysen had called. "Cissy's in the hospital, Martha said. But that's all she knew."

Since the streets were clearer now, Scott decided that it was time for him to leave. He needed to find out more about his cousin. "I'll let you know something as soon as I can," he promised.

———

The next couple of days were much like Tuesday. Schools were closed and churches open to help victims of the storm. Calls were coming in to radio and TV stations from well-wishers all over the nation. Donations of all kinds, including money, began to pour in.

In all, ten people had lost their lives to the killer tornado. Five were still in intensive care at the hospital, and hundreds of others had suffered injuries.

On the third day after the tornado, heavy thunderstorms rolled in and rain again drenched the area. There was still no electricity or working phones. During the day, the older Ainsworths helped at the tornado scene while the younger ones baby-sat with children whose parents were working or were in the hospital. In the evenings, they ate cold food, played games, and counted their blessings.

Near the end of the week, the electricity and phone service were restored. Still, Natalie had heard nothing from Scott. It was Martha Brysen who called to report that Ron was still in the hospital, but that Cissy had been released from the hospital.

Natalie tried to talk herself into believing that there was really no reason for Scott to call. Why should he? Just because they had survived a tornado together didn't mean they were an item!

"I was so excited about a date with Scott. Now going to a play or even the prom seems pretty unimportant."

"Yeah," Ruthie said nonchalantly. "If he asks you for a date, you won't think twice about turning him down, will you?"

"Ach!" Natalie screeched, giving Ruthie a warning

glance. "One of these days I'm gonna strangle you!"

They laughed together before Natalie added seriously, "There was something special between us, though, Ruthie. I guess going through hard times brings people closer."

"It *can*," Ruthie admitted. "I hope it works that way for people who have lost their homes or family members."

In that moment, both girls felt the heaviness some of their more unfortunate neighbors were experiencing.

Then Ruthie brightened, her corkscrew curls bobbing. "But there is one awesome possibility," she suggested. "Maybe we won't have to take finals."

Natalie regarded her friend fondly. "Fat chance of that!"

Eleven

On Sunday, churches throughout the city were packed. Memorial services were held to honor those who had died in the tornado, and prayers were offered for the injured and others left homeless.

School was in session on Monday, with a special class led by a psychologist whose chief purpose was to help students cope with the catastrophe.

Scott stopped Natalie before study hall to report that his cousin and her parents were still trying to come to an understanding and that Ron was improving. "I kind of expected Cissy to be at school today," he said. "Guess she wasn't up to it. Would . . . you go with me to see her after school?" he tacked on hesitantly.

A quick call home confirmed Natalie's hunch that, after the recent ordeal, her parents agreed that she would be safe anywhere with Scott Lambert!

———

Still in the denim skirt and top she had worn to school, Natalie stood with Scott in front of the Stiles's Georgian mansion while he rang the bell. Almost immediately the door was opened by a middle-aged woman in a turquoise uniform. *Must be the maid,* Natalie thought, feeling a little uncomfortable in these lavish surroundings.

"Hello, Mrs. Williams," Scott greeted her warmly. The woman smiled and invited them in.

As soon as Natalie stepped into the spacious foyer, so did Martha Brysen and a tall, elegant couple that Scott introduced as Cissy's parents. They welcomed her as if she were one of Cissy's good friends. Even Martha Brysen was real friendly—much more so, it seemed, than at the meeting at church.

Cissy's mother took both of Natalie's hands in hers. "I'm so glad to meet you, dear. And so thankful you came by to talk to Cissy that terrible night."

Looking on, Mr. Stiles and Martha Brysen nodded in agreement.

Mrs. Stiles' eyes were suspiciously moist as she suggested, "Now, why don't the two of you go on up to Cissy's sitting room? I'll have Cornelia serve some refreshments in a bit."

I guess this is how rich people live, observed Natalie on her way up the ornately carved staircase. *Only three people—and all this room!*

Scott knocked lightly, and Cissy opened the door right away. Natalie breathed a sigh of relief. In her sweats and an old T-shirt, Cissy actually looked pretty ordinary. If she was wearing makeup, it didn't hide the purple bruise on the right side of her face, nor the dark circles under her eyes.

"Thanks for coming, Natalie." Cissy seemed genuinely glad to see her. "I wouldn't have blamed you if you'd never spoken to me again after the way I treated you."

Natalie shrugged. "No big deal. I didn't take it personally."

Cissy frowned a little. "You're really . . . incredible, you know that?"

Embarrassed, Natalie felt her cheeks grow hot. "Oh, believe me, I'm far from perfect. Just ask my sisters!" She glanced at Scott, who was grinning encouragingly.

"We could sit on the veranda, if that's okay." Cissy led the way. "It's a little more private out there."

Following the older girl across the cream-colored carpet, Natalie took a look around. The room was light and airy—and big! Her cubbyhole bedroom over the garage could easily fit into one corner! There was an overstuffed ivory couch and chair, mounded with pastel pillows. In the center of the grouping was a low glass-topped table. One wall consisted of nothing but bookshelves built around a beautiful, old rolltop desk. And on the opposite wall a long, skinny table with gracefully curved legs held a huge arrangement of flowers. Several fine paintings picked up the subdued colors and tied the room together.

Natalie had seen rooms like this before—but only in magazines. Not a thing was out of place. How different from her own home! There, things were rarely in place because there were never enough places!

Still, she was not the least bit envious. As much as Natalie often longed for a little more privacy, she imagined it must be terribly lonely to be an only child, especially when one's parents were always so busy.

She and Scott trailed Cissy onto the veranda—actually a small deck, bordered by a lacy white railing. A wrought-iron table and chairs were grouped comfortably at one end, while potted trees and hanging baskets gave the effect of a garden suspended above the ground.

From the veranda, Natalie could see the swimming pool below and, beyond that, massive shade trees standing guard over the stately old homes in the area. *Scott must live somewhere around here.*

"How's Ron feeling?" she asked Cissy after they pulled up their chairs around the table.

Cissy appeared to be dangerously near tears. "I think he's going to be okay. He had a concussion and three broken ribs. Other than that, just some bruises and minor cuts."

"You were hurt, too—" Natalie began, studying the purplish stain on Cissy's right cheek.

They were interrupted by Mrs. Williams, bringing out a refreshment tray. "Thanks, Cornelia."

"You're entirely welcome, Miss Cissy."

From the strained look on Cissy's face and the pleased one on Cornelia's, Natalie concluded that this was not the usual routine. Cissy must not be used to thanking people for waiting on her.

The small sandwiches and petit fours looked scrumptious, and so did the tall, crystal glasses of lemonade with a lemon slice perched on each rim. Natalie accepted a glass and took a sip, but shook her head when the sandwiches were passed. "I'd like to hear your story first."

Cissy looked up. The blue sky was serene—not a cloud in sight—but her eyes reflected a storm within. "It was the worst, Natalie. I could never have imagined such a thing. My therapist says I need to talk it out. . . . It was like the *Twilight Zone*—or a nightmare—but I couldn't wake up."

Natalie didn't dare glance at Scott or move. She didn't want to break Cissy's concentration.

After a moment, the girl continued. "I kept trying to convince myself and Ron—although he didn't need any convincing—that we were doing the right thing. I was upset because my parents wouldn't let me go into acting," she explained, slumping forward, her head in her hands. She lifted her head. "Now I think I was just trying to strike out at them . . . using Ron as my weapon. Even the wind and the rain seemed to be driving us back, but we pushed ahead anyway."

Cissy seemed to be reliving those moments. "Everything suddenly got very quiet and still. The wind died down, the rain stopped. Then, when Ron turned onto the highway, we saw this huge swirling mass—like black smoke—in the sky. The car was rocking. Other cars were stopping, and people were getting out and running for cover. When the roar of the storm was the loudest, Ron yelled, "I'm outta here!" Then he opened the door and took off . . . without waiting for me." Her voice was a breathless whisper.

Cissy pulled herself together enough to go on. "I don't remember being scared at that moment. All I could think was, 'He ran off and left me. The one I love and want to marry—left me! He's a . . . a coward!'"

Natalie felt the girl's pain as Cissy covered her face with her hands. When she finally moved them away, she looked at Natalie. "I couldn't believe it," she said, a haunted look in her eyes. "The storm didn't matter.

I really didn't care if it swept me away. Nothing could have hurt worse than what Ron had just done to me. . . ."

Natalie and Scott moved their chairs closer while Scott patted Cissy's shoulder awkwardly. She struggled to finish her story. "The wind slammed the car door shut, then picked it up—the whole thing . . . with me inside—and swirled it around and around. I don't know how long I was in that dark funnel. There were other cars . . . and people. I couldn't breathe. . . . Then, just as suddenly as the car had been lifted, it was back on the road again—almost in the exact same spot. It was . . . *weird*!"

In the slight pause that followed, Scott whispered, "Wow!"

Natalie waited, listening.

Cissy went on. Her eyes—like great blue saucers—seemed to be staring into space. "Then I saw the funnel twisting toward the people running for the overpass. Just before Ron reached it, the wind picked him up like—like he was a bird flying through the air, or something. He disappeared into a tree. I heard the limb crack. But I was too scared to look." She squeezed her eyes shut.

"All sorts of things were sailing by. When the . . . the *thing* whirled toward a cluster of houses . . . before it just left . . . I thought I was going out of my mind. . . ."

There was not a sound from Natalie or Scott as they absorbed the horror of what Cissy had seen. Finally Natalie broke the silence. "How did you manage to live through it?"

The tears were rolling down Cissy's cheeks now, leaving a streaky trail of mascara. "I felt something digging into my hand." She reached into her sweats pocket and drew out the little white dove and handed it to Natalie. "When I looked at that pin, I remembered what you had said . . . about asking God for help. Well, I asked Him."

Natalie closed her hand over the little pin and felt the wetness on her own cheeks.

Cissy held her breath, then let it out very slowly. "I felt calmer. I still didn't know what I was going to do, but I knew I wasn't alone. It felt like God reached down and gave me a good shaking, but . . . He saved my life."

Cissy smiled and dabbed at her teary face with a fresh tissue she dug out of her other pocket. "When the storm was over, I tried to find Ron. But it was getting too dark to see. And there were no lights on anywhere. I turned the car back toward town and, as I did, the headlights lit up the neighborhood across the street. Except"—her face mirrored the shock she was still feeling—"there were no houses there anymore!" she blurted out. "Just a big pile of wood and bricks. I could hear people moaning and calling for help. But I couldn't move. Then I heard the sirens. A police car pulled up beside me, and an officer told me to go on home. But I couldn't find . . . home. . . ." Her whispery voice trailed off altogether.

"Oh, Cissy!" Natalie reached out and touched the girl's bare arm. It felt cold and clammy.

"I've heard a lot of strange stories this week," Scott said, shaking his head. "But nothing like this."

"There were no house lights," Cissy continued after a moment, "no streetlights, nothing but pitch-black darkness. I got off the main road as soon as I could—to let the emergency vehicles through. A couple of times I thought I recognized a landmark. But when I got closer, it was gone." She gulped.

"Finally I saw a bright light and headed for it. It turned out to be a church, setting up to help people in trouble after the storm. People like *me*. So I asked a man where Garden Acres was. He told me it was just a few blocks up the street. And then . . . *all* the lights went out!"

Scott and Natalie looked at each other, then took Cissy's cold hands to let her know they cared.

"I guess I fainted, because when I came to, I was in the hospital—with *this* shiner." She touched the purplish smudge on her cheek and winced. "I had to wait my turn, though, because the more serious injuries were treated first."

When she wound down at last, Natalie let out a breath. "What a story!"

But Cissy wasn't through. "The whole time, I never let go of the little white dove." She turned to Natalie, gazing at her intently. "If it's some kind of special club . . . I'd like to join."

Twelve

By Wednesday, the buzz at school had begun to die down. At basketball practice that afternoon, however, Stick outdid himself and scored five three-pointers. This extraordinary achievement replaced talk of the tornado at youth group meeting that night.

Even Andy brought it up in his kick-off remarks. "We always have a short business meeting before our Bible study," he explained to Cissy and Scott, who had come at Natalie's invitation to learn more about the White Dove program. "But first, I'd like to congratulate Stick on those three-pointers today."

There was wild clapping, with a few piercing whistles thrown in. Stick stood and bowed dramatically. "To tell the truth, it's because I was upset," he admitted, his face flaming. "The school has set up a lot of ball practices for Wednesday nights. I tried to talk the principal into changing it to another night. Even said I'd get up a petition. But he said the summer sessions have to be set up to suit the leaders, not the students, and it just wasn't 'feasible' to change it. Said if they do that for a church group, they'd have to do the same for other groups."

"Good try," Andy commended him. "Anyone else got any ideas?"

There was not a sound in the room.

Stick stumbled over his chair, then mumbled, "If we can't change the practice night, maybe we could change our meeting night."

Still no one spoke up.

He shrugged, straightened his chair, held on to it carefully, and slouched down into it. "I know, I know. We have to meet on Wednesday night. We have to please the grown-ups."

"Now, hold on, Stick," Andy said thoughtfully. "You may have something there. No, we probably can't change church family night, but we could set up another time for our White Dove meetings instead of combining them with Wednesday night Bible study."

"There's never a school practice on *Friday* night," Evelyn suggested, then her face fell. "But that's a date night."

"Well, criminy! Who cares!" Stick complained.

Ruthie shot him a dangerous glare. "Plenty of us care. Besides, you just had a date yourself not long ago."

"Yeah, I liked it so much I might even have another one next year!" he piped up, enjoying the hoots that followed.

"Hey," Ruthie persisted, "Friday might be a great night. Some of us could bring our dates."

There were a few gasps.

"Well," she said huffily, "whoever gripes about having a date at church isn't the right person to be going out with anyhow!"

"*Every* Friday night we're going to bring our date to church?" someone moaned.

"Not every week," Stephanie put in. "We *will* need to meet pretty regularly until we've planned the Sunday morning service for the White Dove ceremony. After that, it'll be up to you how often we meet and what you want to discuss at those meetings."

"Sure," Andy agreed. "We might have a program on AIDS one week, then repeat it a couple of weeks later. That way, everyone would have a chance to hear the discussion, and it would still leave time for other activities."

"Sounds okay to me."

"Yeah . . . maybe."

"Guess so."

Andy stood in front of the group, his arms folded. "I think I hear you saying that you're willing to give it a try. Any more thoughts on the subject?"

"For once, Stick came up with a great idea," Ruthie commented, adding under her breath, "although it's probably his *last*."

Just as he stuck out his tongue at her, Amy looked his way. "I don't have cheerleading practice or anything on Fridays, so I could come every time."

Stick retrieved his tongue, nearly swallowed it, and sat up straighter in his chair. Natalie couldn't help chuckling. The poor guy probably couldn't believe Amy had agreed with him.

He leaned over Ruthie to speak to Amy. "If you want me to, I'll even ask your sister out again."

Amy groaned, and Ruthie hit Stick on the top of the head with her notepad. "Get outta here, you dork!"

In response, Stick jumped up, did a few shuffle steps as he dribbled an imaginary basketball, then arced a perfect shot toward the trash can in the corner. "Another three-pointer!"

"Why don't you take a hyper pill?" Ruthie gibed.

"If you'll take an ugly pill!" he retorted.

"Did you hear that? He's saying I'm pretty!"

"Pretty ugly and pretty apt to stay that way!"

"Okay, okay," Stephanie intervened, stepping up beside Andy, "enough fun and games. It's time to get down to business." She began to explain the White Dove program to the newcomers, including the plans for a worship service for the entire church.

As the meeting progressed and Scott asked questions about the program, Natalie was reminded of the devastating events of the past week. It was obvious that some good was already coming out of it. A lot of people—including some of her new friends—were taking their spiritual lives more seriously.

She still didn't know much about Scott, but she had learned a lot about Cissy in the past few days, and she was definitely different. In fact, she and Scott were talking about starting a group like White Dove at their own church.

Natalie wasn't surprised to hear Andy say that the ceremony would include a commitment to sexual abstinence. After all, White Dove had been inspired by a program based on that aspect of one's life. Nor was she surprised when none of the guys rose to the challenge of giving a personal testimony.

But she *was* surprised when, a few days later, Andy told the group that Scott Lambert had asked to speak at their special ceremony. "He wanted to know if anyone would mind since he's not a member of our church. But I told him that if he's a member of God's family, he's automatically a part of ours."

———

The day of the ceremony dawned sunny and bright. The church was packed. The youth group—plus the special speakers, including Scott Lambert and Cissy Stiles—were crammed into the front pews.

Pastor Darlee opened with prayer and then turned the service over to Andy and Stephanie. Natalie was always impressed with the Kellys' teamwork. Speaking alternately, they explained the program that had come to be called the White Dove Movement, telling how teens were committing themselves to learning to show love for others in obedience to Jesus' command.

Cissy was next. Natalie had heard Cissy preside over the student council meetings many times, but she wasn't sure what to expect today.

The tall girl glided to the podium. Dressed in a summer sheath, Cissy was as poised and beautiful as ever, spotlighted in the shaft of sunlight that poured through the stained-glass window of the church. But this time Natalie noticed something different about her—something warm and open—a glow that didn't have anything to do with the girl's perfect features or where she was standing at the moment.

"It took a tornado to blow some sense into my head," Cissy began. "While all the elements were raging, I was hanging on to this little white dove in my hand." She held it up, although it was too tiny to be seen beyond the first row. "It's just a pretty little ornament that left its imprint on my palm. But the dove reminded me that God's Spirit wants to leave His imprint on my heart. I felt His presence that night. Only *He* could have reached into that funnel and brought me safely through," she choked. "I don't know why He spared my life, except that He had a reason. Now I've rededicated myself to serving Him and trusting those around me who are wiser than I am."

Her voice quavered when she mentioned Ron. "My boyfriend was caught up in the tornado . . . and I couldn't find him for a long time. But I found something more important—a deeper relationship with the Lord. Maybe it would have happened without this little pin. But it didn't." She caught Natalie's eye and smiled. "A friend gave me this pin to remind me where to turn in times of trouble. And He didn't let me down."

She paused, then straightened her shoulders, her voice clear and firm. "I've come home—back to my parents and back to God. I still have some nightmares, and I'm sad because the relationship with my boyfriend is no longer the same. But I feel good, too. I believe God will lead me into the right career. But I don't feel like I have to be in a hurry anymore. If it isn't His plan, then I don't want it."

Someone in the back began clapping, timidly at first. Then a few others joined in until everyone was applauding. This was pretty unusual for her church, Natalie knew. But some of them had lost loved ones in the tornado. And others still had family members in the hospital, recovering from injuries. Cissy had obviously helped them remember that God was with them, too, in the grief and trouble that had followed in the wake of that deadly storm.

Natalie walked forward and stepped up to the podium. She opened her Bible. "I'm reading from Matthew 3:16–17, the New International Version: 'As soon as Jesus was baptized, he went up out of the water. At that moment heaven was open and he saw the Spirit of God descending like a dove and lighting on him. And a voice from heaven said, "This is my Son, whom I love; with him I am well pleased." ' "

She closed the Bible. "The very next verse talks about the temptations Jesus faced. As we've been learning in youth Bible study, sometimes when we're closest to God, the devil works the hardest to lure us away. So as we commit ourselves to God today, we shouldn't be surprised if we're tempted as soon as we leave here. Like Jesus, though, we have God's Spirit to guide us and give us strength to overcome temptation."

She returned to her seat on the front row, passing Scott, who gave her a smile on his way to the podium. He looked so cool in his navy blazer and khakis.

He gripped the edges of the pulpit and looked down as if searching for words, then he lifted his head. "Everything was going great until a couple of years ago when my world was blown apart, a lot like the devastation caused by that tornado last week. We moved away from the school and friends who had been a big part of my life, and I got into a lot of things I shouldn't have. Sometimes I even wondered if life was worth living." He dropped his head and hunched his shoulders forward.

Scott Lambert? Natalie thought. *The guy who has it all—good looks, money—even a genuine faith in God?* But then, he wasn't a bit cocky about any of it. Instead, he was willing to humble himself before a church full of people, including practically half the population of Shawnee High!

He straightened and looked out over the congregation. "When there was nothing else to do, nowhere else to go, I turned to God. I wasn't sure He could use my life—what was left of it—but I offered it to Him all the same. He took me up on my offer. And gradually, He gave me the will to live again and to make something of my life." He paused before going on. "But that wasn't the end." Scanning the front row, Scott's gaze found and locked with Natalie's. "Like the scripture Natalie read says, it was just the beginning—like a test to see if I meant what I had said."

A wry smile tugged at the corners of his mouth. "As soon as I started talking about this program with the guys at school, I began to get a lot of flak. More than one ridiculed me for even thinking about taking a vow to abstain from sex. 'You don't know what you're missing, man,' they said."

Natalie held her breath, waiting to hear what Scott would say next.

"Well, I *do* know what I'm missing. I'm missing venereal disease. I'm missing AIDS. I'm missing teen pregnancy. I'm missing guilt. And I'm missing God's disapproval."

A hush fell over the congregation. Tentatively at first, as before, then more vigorously, applause broke out and continued for a full minute. Mrs. Brysen, who was sitting on the fourth row, stood, still clapping. She was joined by Mrs. Johnson and Jim Parill. One by one, the entire congregation rose to pay tribute to Scott for his courage and willingness to speak out.

Natalie grinned. The applause seemed like a hearty endorsement of the White Dove program—and the whole youth group!

The sound echoed from the vaulted ceiling as Scott left the podium and took his seat, to be replaced by a small group of young people, including Ruthie, who stood in front of a microphone at the front. Their voices blended in harmony as they sang "On the Wings of a Dove" while the others filed to the front to sign a huge poster dominated by a large white bird. By the time Andy closed the service with a prayer of commitment, Natalie could see that other faces were reflecting what she felt—pure joy.

———

The Stiles took the Ainsworths to the country club for dinner after church—everyone, that is, except Jim Ainsworth, who was working the Sunday shift at the prison, and Dr. Lambert, who had a meeting of the hospital staff.

Over dessert, Martha Brysen announced, "I've told Andy and Stephanie that I'll fund all the white doves they need to distribute for the program. And I hope there will be a whole flock!"

Catching the twinkle in the woman's eye, Natalie was no longer apprehensive. Behind that facade of cool confidence, she realized, was a sweet spirit. Relieved, Natalie joined in the ripple of laughter around the table.

"My dad should be home by now," Scott told Natalie on the way to his house from the country club. "I've been wanting the two of you to meet. I've told him all about you." He slanted her a warm smile.

She felt her cheeks go red, wishing she didn't always give away her emotions so easily. At least she'd get to see where Scott lived. "You . . . never mention your mom. Will I get to meet her, too?"

There was a guarded look on his face. "I never talk about her."

Oh, brother! Natalie thought. *Why did I have to mention his mother? I've gone and spoiled everything!*

To her immense relief, he smiled again. "But if I'm ever able to open up about her, I'd like it to be with *you*, Nat."

His gaze held a warmth that tingled through her like a Fourth-of-July sparkler. She couldn't take her eyes off him.

Turning at the curb in front of his house, he pulled over and killed the engine. But he made no move to get out of the car. She waited, almost afraid to breathe.

"We've come through a lot together, Natalie."

"I . . . I've learned a lot, too, Scott. When I first met you, and Cissy said you might ask me to the prom—"

She broke off when he thundered, "*What?*"

Natalie threw up her hands and laughed nervously. "Oh, it's okay. It's really okay."

"No, it's not." A muscle flexed in his jaw. "If I'd known what Cissy told you, I would have explained. I *wanted* to ask you—you seemed like the kind of person

I'd like to be with. Cissy knew you from student council and thought we'd hit it off. But my dad found out that he could get away the weekend of the prom, and we had to visit my mother."

"Visit . . . your mother?" she echoed.

Scott turned his head and looked out through the windshield. "Maybe someday I can tell you about it, Natalie."

Apparently Scott's mom didn't live in Garden City. It was all more mysterious than ever. *Help me, Lord, to be the kind of friend who loves with your kind of love—pure love.*

Then, before she knew it, he had grabbed her hands and was leaning over to kiss her cheek. "Let's go meet my dad."

She floated from the car, hoping the spot on her cheek was not glowing a fiery red. It sure felt like it! The walkway to the house felt like a cloud, or else her feet weren't really touching the pavement. Or maybe, she thought, just maybe, it was the flutter of the little dove's wings, reminding her to keep her feet on the ground!

———

What distressing secret is Scott Lambert hiding? Can he open his heart to Natalie? And what temptations will they both face when Natalie spends a week at the Lamberts' Lake Oakwood summer cottage? Don't miss the intriguing answers in WHITE DOVE ROMANCE #2, *Secret Storm!*